Routledge Revivals

Sea Serpents, Sailors & Sceptics

Originally published in 1978 *Sea Serpents, Sailors and Sceptics* looks at stories of folklore and mythology which have fascinated sailors from antiquity to the modern day. From stories of large unauthenticated sea creatures to the Loch Ness Monster, documented sightings are vast and the book provides a concise survey and review of the subject of ocean folklore. It shows how some large sea creatures, such as the giant squid, have been established and addresses some of the explanations of sea serpents and other sea creatures as now known, categorised species and offers a classification of these species that have formulated the mythologies of the sea throughout time. The book discusses how relatively little is known about the sea still and offers a practical look at the possibility that these mythological creatures, might in fact be, as yet undiscovered species. This book provides a unique interdisciplinary volume, crossing between the area of literature and folklore, and natural historians alike, and will appeal to academics working in the field of natural history and folklore alike.

Sea Serpents, Sailors & Sceptics

by Graham J. McEwan

Routledge
Taylor & Francis Group

REVIVALS

First published in 1978
by Routledge & Kegan Paul Ltd,

This edition first published in 2018 by Routledge
2 Park Square, Milton Park, Abingdon, Oxon, OX14 4RN
and by Routledge
711 Third Avenue, New York, NY 10017

Routledge is an imprint of the Taylor & Francis Group, an informa business

© 1978 Graham J. McEwan

Publisher's Note
The publisher has gone to great lengths to ensure the quality of this reprint but points out that some imperfections in the original copies may be apparent.

Disclaimer
The publisher has made every effort to trace copyright holders and welcomes correspondence from those they have been unable to contact.
A Library of Congress record exists under LCCN: 0710089317

ISBN 13: 978-0-367-07728-0 (hbk)
ISBN 13: 978-0-429-02243-2 (ebk)
ISBN 13: 978-0-367-07735-8 (pbk)

Sea Serpents, Sailors and Sceptics

Sea Serpents, Sailors and Sceptics

Graham J.McEwan

Routledge & Kegan Paul

London, Henley and Boston

First published in 1978
by Routledge & Kegan Paul Ltd
39 Store Street,
London WC1E 7DD,
Broadway House,
Newtown Road,
Henley-on-Thames,
Oxon RG9 1EN and
9 Park Street,
Boston, Mass. 02108, USA
Set in 11/12pt Baskerville by
Express Litho Service (Oxford)

British Library Cataloguing in Publication Data

McEwan, Graham J

Sea serpents, sailors and sceptics.
1. Sea monsters
I. Title
001.9'44   OL89.2.S4   78-40159

ISBN 0 7100 8931 7

Contents

Plates

Figures

Acknowledgments

I would like to thank the following for permission to reproduce photographs: Mrs M. M. Smith, plate 2; the *Illustrated London News*, plates 3 and 4; Ardea Wildlife Photographic Library and E. Mickleburgh, plate 5; the American Museum of Natural History, plate 6; Tony 'Doc' Shiels, plates 11, 12, and 13.

I would also like to thank the following for permission to quote excerpts: Tim Dinsdale and Futura publications, for *The Leviathans*; the *Daily Telegraph*; the *Orcadian*; *Cornish Life* magazine.

I am grateful for assistance from the following: Tim Dinsdale; David Clarke, editor of *Cornish Life* magazine; Tony 'Doc' Shiels; Ray Manners of *Info* magazine; F. W. Holliday; Bob Bird, photographer; The British Museum; Bob Rickard, Editor of *Fortean Times*; Radcliffe Science Library, Oxford.

ONE
The Case for Sea Serpents

Many creatures whose existence is now firmly established were, a couple of hundred years ago, nothing more than legends and, as the years have passed, various bizarre and improbable creatures have been slowly, often almost grudgingly accepted by the scientific establishment. Many such creatures are marine, one of the most spectacular being the giant squid, which was largely regarded as a mythical beast until the middle of the nineteenth century. This book is based on the six hundred reported sightings of large unknown sea creatures – popularly known as sea serpents – in the past two hundred years. Excluding hoaxes (these being easily identifiable), mistakes, and even merely doubtful sightings we are left with nearly four hundred apparently genuine reports. These reports are trustworthy, not merely because of the obvious good faith and reliability of the witnesses, but because of the consistency of their descriptions, the same details appearing year after year, century after century. Often the creatures were seen by many people simultaneously, such as ships' crews and the passengers of liners, all of whose accounts agree on the main features. The time for which the animals were under observation varies from a few minutes up to half an hour, and sometimes longer. The witnesses cannot be accused of being sensation seekers, for many of them kept silent for years about their encounters with sea serpents, fearing, with good reason, that they would be ridiculed. Those who did relate their experiences were, indeed, often treated with scorn.

1

Even those who have accepted the existence of sea serpents have often confused the issue by maintaining, quite against the evidence, that there is only one type of sea serpent, usually insisting that it is a surviving species of giant reptile from a past epoch. As we shall see, all the evidence points to there being several types of sea serpent, most of which exhibit characteristics which are definitely mammalian. The believers, in fact, have weakened their own case by arguing on a biologically unsound basis.

Most people are unaware of the great number of sightings of sea serpents, as indeed I was before studying the subject. Many accounts appear in old books, small regional newspapers, and defunct natural history journals, and it is unfortunate that the most dubious accounts — some blatant hoaxes — have often received the widest publicity.

Attempts have been made to dismiss sea serpents as sightings of known phenomena. The inadequacy of such explanations will become obvious to the reader, but it is probably advisable to clear the decks before we start. It has been suggested that the animal seen, and described as a sea serpent, was really a large land snake swimming far from land. Now snakes are good swimmers and some of the larger species are known to make short trips in coastal waters. A 30-foot python would make an impressive spectacle swimming in the sea and its size could easily be exaggerated. However, on land or in water, snakes can move only by *undulating in a horizontal plane.* This sideways movement is characteristic of cold-blooded creatures such as fish and reptiles. All the sea serpents seen swimming by undulating their bodies have done so in a *vertical plane,* which is characteristic of mammals. These two different modes of progression are the result of basic differences in the anatomy of cold-blooded and hot-blooded animals, and the importance of this point is often not appreciated. Also, it is highly unlikely that land snakes could make their way into the middle of oceans where many of the sightings occur.

Another suggestion is that schools of porpoises swimming in single file may have been mistaken for one long sea monster. Many witnesses say that this was the first thought that entered their heads, but that they immediately discounted it on seeing a long neck held 15 feet [4.5 metres] or so out of the water, or a row of humps that were visibly joined.

One of the most popular theories put forward is that the sea serpent is really an oarfish. This is a large serpentine fish with two long, oar-shaped pectoral fins, from which its name is derived. Little is known about this fish, which seldom appears on the surface, most of our knowledge coming from specimens washed ashore during storms. The largest known oarfish was that washed ashore at Newport Beach, California, in 1901 (see plate 1) which was 21 feet [6.3 metres] long, and such lengths are rare. Of course, like all fish, it moves by undulating sideways, and so cannot be claimed as a sea serpent.

These are the more reasonable suggestions put forward to explain away sea serpents. Just about every large sea animal, whatever its shape, has been advanced at one time or another. Some theories even suggest phenomena such as a flight of birds near the surface of the water, or elongated masses of seaweed. However, all these theories, which might explain some of the more doubtful reports, do not account for those features repeatedly described – the long necks held high out of water, the vertical undulations, the rows of humps, and the high speeds attained by the beasts, which often throw up a wash visible at a great distance.

The sceptics' classic argument is 'We'll accept the sea serpent when we have the body of one.' In fact, over the years, there have been many puzzling carcases netted or washed ashore, and while most of them turn out to be the remains of known creatures there are several which remain unidentified to this day.

Further, many sea creatures are known only from one or two specimens and several (mainly of the whale family) are known *only* from eye witness accounts and yet accepted by science. Here are details of some of them:

In the early nineteenth century the naturalist Samuel Constantin Rafinesque published an account of an unknown species of whale with two dorsal fins, a very strange feature, which had been sighted by the naturalist Antonino Mongitore. This was later confirmed by Quoy and Gaimard who saw a whole school of them between the Sandwich Islands and New South Wales. A specimen was never caught, nor were its remains ever washed up, but it was accepted by scientists and named *Delphinus rhinoceros*.

An unknown species of whale with a very high dorsal fin has been reported around the Shetlands over the years, one of the witnesses being Robert Sibbald, an authority on whales. It is some 60 feet [18 metres] long, has been named *Physeter tursio* and no one has secured a fragment of it.

The famous naturalist Philip Gosse once spent several hours watching an unknown species of whale in the North Atlantic. The whales were some 30 feet [9 metres] long with pink snouts. No specimen has been obtained, but Gosse was not called a liar or a crank, perhaps because whales are a 'respectable' family, unlike sea serpents.

The opinions of many orthodox scientists were altered by the capture in 1939 of a live coelacanth (see plate 2) a large predatory fish which was thought to have become extinct 70 million years ago, there being no fossil evidence after this time. Professor J. L. B. Smith, who examined the fish and established its identity, was frankly disbelieved by many naturalists who did not even trouble to go and see the remains, one maintaining that the fish was merely a common rock cod with a deformed tail! More coelacanths have been caught since, one on a rod and line at a depth of only 50 feet [15 metres], thus refuting the common fallacy that unknown creatures must inhabit only abyssal depths. If the coelacanth could survive for so long so could other creatures from that and succeeding periods, the sea presenting one of the most favourable environments changing little over millions of years.

Some reports speak of sea serpents up to 250 feet [75 metres] long, and although this is almost certainly an exaggeration, such a size is not impossible. The largest whales are about 100 feet [30 metres] long and weigh about 160 tons. A long, slender sea creature of 250 feet [75 metres] would probably weigh less than this and the sea is a suitable medium for giantism. Many of the largest sea beasts have been discovered in comparatively recent years and are still rather mysterious.

The largest known fish – the whale shark – may reach a length of 60 feet [18 metres] and was not discovered until 1829.

The largest ray – the manta ray – was not discovered until 1830 and may be 24 feet [7.2 metres] across.

The dwarf cachalot, of the sperm whale family, was described from skeletal remains in 1846. It is 10 feet [3 metres] long and no live ones have ever been seen.

Despite its name, the pygmy whale may attain lengths of 60 feet [18 metres]. It is very rarely seen and was not known before 1864.

Little is known about the beaked whales, or *Ziphiidae* and in 1937 a new genus had to be created when three specimens of an unknown type were washed ashore in New Zealand. They were nearly 30 feet [9 metres] long. Two more species of the *Ziphiidae* are Arnoux's whale, first described in 1851, and Baird's whale first described in 1883. They are about 40 feet [12 metres] long and Baird's whale has erectile teeth set in cartilaginous sacs, a completely un-mammalian characteristic. One of the rarest of the group is Gervais's whale, discovered in 1840, of which only six specimens have been found.

Despite great advances in all branches of science we still know relatively little about the sea, whose average depth is 11,000 feet [3,300 metres], sinking to 30,000 feet [9,000 metres] in places – six miles [9.5 kilometres] deep. It covers three-fifths of the earth's surface, and the proportion frequented by shipping is tiny, being restricted to the established lanes. Also, the world's fishing fleets are almost entirely confined to the northern hemisphere, fishing in the southern hemisphere, which contains the bulk of the world's ocean, being almost negligible. The very nature of this huge volume of water makes exploration difficult if not impossible, and inevitably we can only know a fraction of its fauna.

5

TWO
The Nineteenth Century I

One of the earliest references to sea serpents seems to be that of Aristotle who writes of animals in the sea which

> cannot be classified by kind because they are too rare. Among the fishermen with long experience, some claim to have seen in the sea animals like beams of wood, black, round and the same thickness throughout. Others of these animals are like shields: they are said to be red in colour and have many fins.

Aristotle was also the first scientist to dissect squids and he talks of giant squids, of which we shall hear more later. From here on we have only isolated, confused and vague reports, which frequently combine real and mythical creatures in the most fantastic ways. Also, of course, many early reports have been lost through the passage of time. The situation does not improve until the latter half of the eighteenth century, when the world was opened up by trade and exploration, resulting in a great increase in sightings. Also, people's treatment of the subject became more scientific.

I propose to start the story in the early nineteenth century in the waters of New England, where sea serpents were seen continually, ranging from Gloucester Bay, Massachusetts, up to Long Island. In 1817 the sightings became a frequent, almost daily occurrence and among the first witnesses were two women and several fishermen who, on 6 August, saw a

7

huge, many-humped creature swim into the harbour of Cape Ann, just north of Gloucester Roads. Four days later a similar beast – maybe even the same creature – appeared near Ten Pound Island, where it was seen from the mainland by Amos Story, a sailor. On 14 August it was watched by a crowd of some thirty people, including the Justice of the Peace, Lonson Nash. From then on it was seen repeatedly and was excitedly discussed in the local press, the Boston *Weekly Messenger* carrying a series of detailed accounts. Word soon reached the Linnean Society of New England, who met at Boston to form a committee of enquiry. The committee had three members — Judge John Davis, Dr Jacob Bigelow, and naturalist Francis Grey. The committee asked Lonson Nash to collect sworn statements from those who had obtained a good view of the monster.

While Nash went about his work the creature continued to show itself. On 16 August it was seen by Colonel Parkin and Mr Lee from the shore and at the same time by the captain and crew of a nearby ship. It was observed several times further out at sea by various ships, including a revenue cutter. Nash undertook his task thoroughly and objectively, first asking witnesses to describe what they had seen and recording their descriptions, and then putting to them a series of questions devised by the Linnean Society. Eleven detailed affidavits were collected, eight from Gloucester and three from Boston.

From these reports which were very consistent, the appearance of the animal can be deduced. It was about 65 feet [19.5 metres] long, over a foot [30 centimentres] wide, and showed a series of humps, the number of which varied slightly. It could move very quickly, speeds of 30 to 70 knots being given, but obviously the latter figure is an exaggeration, speed in water being very difficult to estimate. It did not seem to be bothered by close human company, not even when someone took a shot at it.

The animal reappeared in Gloucester Bay the following year. There were several sightings and, on 29 July, a boat-load of men set out to pursue the beast with muskets. The creature seemed to be playing on the surface and received several shots without the slightest concern. The following day

Captain Webber approached within 2 or 3 metres and hurled a harpoon at it. The harpoon bounced off and the animal immediately dived, nearly swamping the boat as it did so. After this the monster left the area for a while but was seen by several people at Salem, 12 miles [19 kilometres] away. It soon returned to Gloucester Bay, though, and was seen on 12 August by four men in a boat from about 10 yards [9 metres] away, and they give a clear description:

> His head was elevated from three to five feet; the distance was about six feet from his neck to the first bunch [hump] we counted twenty bunches, and we supposed them on average about five feet apart, and his whole length could not be less than one hundred and twenty feet. . . . His head was of a dark brown colour, formed like a seal's and shined with a glossy appearance. . . . His body was of the size of a sixty or eighty gallon cask, his head as large as a barrel for we could see it when he was about four miles from us. I believe he is perfectly harmless, and might easily be caught. . . . There was nothing that appeared like fins or gills. We did not discern his tail. There was a quick vibration of the parts we saw, which was probably his mode of swimming.

On 19 August the monster appeared near Squam Lighthouse in Gloucester Bay and several whaleboats set out in pursuit. They chased the beast for several hours, and eventually Captain Rich harpooned the animal as it swam underneath his boat. The beast immediately shot off, dragging the boat with it until it freed itself from the harpoon.

In the summer of the following year, 1819, the sea serpent returned to Massachusetts. On 13 August it was watched by a crowd of some two hundred people, one of whom was James Prince, Marshall of the district, who gave the following description: 'His head appeared about three feet out of the water; I counted thirteen bunches on his back: my family thought there were fifteen . . . and judged he was fifty feet in length, and at the extend not more than sixty.'

Figure 1 The Massachusetts sea serpent, after James Prince

On 26 August, the Rev. Cheever Felch sent an account to the Boston *Sentinal* of a monster he had seen from the schooner *Science,* which was surveying Gloucester Harbour that morning.

> We had a good view of him, except the very short period while he was under water for half an hour.
> His colour is a dark brown, with white under the throat. His size, we could not accurately ascertain, but his head is about three feet in circumference, flat and much smaller than his body. We did not see his tail; but from the end of the head to the fartherest protuberance, was not far from one hundred feet. I speak with a degree of certainty, from being much accustomed to measure and estimate distances and length. I counted fourteen bunches on his back, the first one, say ten or twelve feet from his head, and the others about seven feet apart. They decreased in size towards the tail. These bunches were sometimes counted with, and sometimes without a glass. Mr. Malbone counted thirteen, Mr. Blake thirteen and fourteen, and the boatman about the same number.
> His motion was sometimes very rapid, and at other times he lay nearly still. He turned slowly, and took up considerable room in doing it. He sometimes darted under the water, with the greatest velocity, as if seizing prey. The protuberances were not from his motion, as they were the same whether in slow or rapid movement.

As this report points out, the humps along the back of the New England sea serpent are far too small and numerous to be undulations in the creature's spine. They are static and apparently solid.

10

For several years after its initial appearance at Gloucester Bay, the sea serpent was seen off New England, mainly off the shores of Massachusetts. In August 1820 it was seen from Phillips Beach, Swampscott, Mass., by Andrew Reynolds and three friends, who managed to launch a rowing boat and approach to within 30 yards [27 metres] of it.

> He had a head about two feet long, and shaped like an egg, which he carried out of the water when he was moving. There were several protuberances on his back, the highest points of which appeared to be seven or eight inches above the level of the water. He was completely black.

A report of the many-humped sea serpent in July 1823 is particularly interesting in that it mentions the beast's vertical undulations: 'It stood eastwardly, at the rate of five miles an hour, with an undulating motion, like that of a caterpillar.' Vertical undulations, which appear in some invertebrates, are also a characteristic of mammals. All reptiles, fish, and amphibians undulate in a horizontal plane.

While the many-humped sea serpents were appearing so regularly off the American coast, sea serpents were being reported on the other side of the Atlantic, in the seas and fjords of Norway. These beasts had been seen during the eighteenth century, but the reports were rather vague and often clouded with superstition, though Hans Egede and Pastor Bing have left us an interesting sketch of a monster that they had seen off Greenland in 1734 (see figure 2). However, in the early nineteenth century there are ten clear reports painstakingly collected by Sir Arthur de Capelle Brooke, who, while travelling through Norway, recorded as much information as he could muster on the sea serpents. He gave details in his fascinating book *Travels through Norway, Sweden and Finmark during the Summer of 1820,* published in 1823.

One of the first witnesses Sir Arthur encountered was Captain Schilderup, who told him of the beast that appeared off the island of Otersun, Hordaland, in 1819. The summer that year was unusually hot and sultry and the beast was seen

11

every day on the surface of the water, apparently basking in the sun. The entire population of Otersun, some thirty people, went to view the creature, which Schilderup said was grey, over 100 feet [30 metres] long and showed several undulations of its great body above water. In August, when the creature appeared in Vegafjord, Nordland, a fisherman, John Gregor, described it as being greyish and showing several large coils on the surface. On two occasions the creatures were seen in pairs, the first time by the Bishop of Nordland and Finmark, who had seen the two beasts swimming together off Trondhjem, Tröndelag, some years previously. He said that they were about 100 feet [30 metres] long and dark grey. A pair was also seen by the skipper of a fishing boat in 1820, off Hundholm, Tröndelag. Like other witnesses he described them as grey in colour and showing several big curves of their serpentine bodies.

From the above descriptions we can see that this type of sea serpent is very different from that seen off North America. It is considerably larger, its length often being given as over 100 feet [30 metres], is grey in colour, rather than the blackish brown of the American type, and shows several big coils above water. These coils are undulations of the flexible spine, and are quite different from the many small, apparently solid humps on the back of the New England sea serpents. Sir Arthur sums up:

> The simple facts are these: in traversing a space full 700 miles of coast, extending to the most northern point, accounts have been received from numerous persons respecting the appearance of an animal, called by them a sea serpent. This of itself would induce some degree of credit to be given to it; but when these several relations as to the general appearance of the animal, its dimensions, the state of the weather when it was seen, and other particulars, are so fully confirmed, one by the other, at such considerable intervening distances, every reasonable man will feel satisfied of the main fact. Many of the informants, besides, were of superior rank and education; and the opinions of such men as the Armstrand (governor) of Finmark, Mr. Steen of Carsloe, Prosten (Dean) Deinbolt

of Vadsoe, and the Bishop of Nordland and Finmark, who was even an eye witness, ought not to be disregarded. There does not appear the least probability, or even possibility, that any other marine animal, at present known on the Northern coast, could have been confounded with the sea serpent.

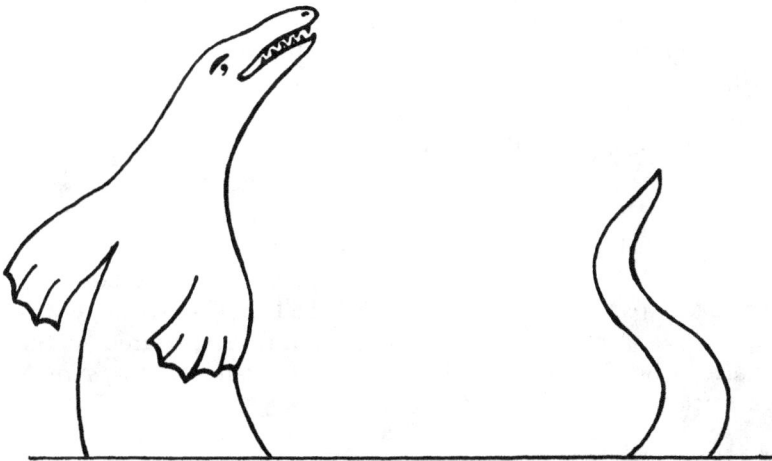

Figure 2   Hans Egede's sea serpent, after Pastor Bing

Although sightings continued in Scandinavian waters the reports became vague and isolated, but frequent and detailed reports continued from the North American coast. On 23 March 1830 the schooner *Eagle* encountered a strange beast about a mile from Simon's Bay, South Carolina. At about 11 o'clock that morning Captain Deland saw a huge animal swimming along about 300 yards [270 metres] from the ship, which approached to within 25 yards [22.5 metres] of the beast. The captain fired his musket at the animal, which immediately dived under the boat, striking it several times with its tail in an alarming way. The captain and the crew all obtained a good view of the animal, which was about 70 feet [21 metres] long, dark in colour, and with a row of humps along its back. The men also saw a smaller specimen further off, which was soon joined by the larger one, seemingly unharmed by the shot. An account of the incident appeared in a German scientific journal *Notizen aus dem Gebiete der Natur- und Heilkunde,* showing how the fame, and respectability, of the American sea serpents had increased.

In March 1835, the brig *Mangehan* arrived at Gloucester Harbour, with a report of a sea monster the crew had seen about 10 miles [16 kilometres] from the Race Point Light. Captain Shibbles said that the beast's head was as large as a barrel, held about 8 feet [2.4 metres] out of the water and with some sort of mane on its neck. He also said that the eyes were huge. The mane and prominent eyes seem to set this creature apart from the typical New England sea serpent, of which we now have a report from the geologist J. W. Dawson.

In 1846 J. W. Dawson was travelling in the USA with the famous geologist Sir Charles Lyell, and he recorded an account of a sea serpent which appeared off the coast of Arisaig, Nova Scotia, in October 1844. The witness was Mr Barry, a millwright, whose description appeared in Sir Charles's book *A Second Visit to the United States of North America,* published in 1850. Barry

> told Mr Dawson he was within 120 feet of it, and estimated its length at sixty feet, and the thickness of its body at three feet. It had humps on the back, which seemed too small and close together to be bends of the body.
>
> The body appeared also to move in long undulations, including many of the smaller humps. In consequence of this action, the head and tail were sometimes both out of sight, and sometimes both above water. . . . The head was rounded and obtuse in front, and was never elevated more than a foot above the surface.

Once again a witness has shown that the humps on the North American sea serpent are too small and numerous to be undulations in the spine, and that the body as a whole moves with long vertical undulations.

In the summer of 1846 there was a dramatic reappearance of the beast with the mane and bulging eyes, which was seen by James Wilson and James Boehner from a schooner in

St Margaret's Bay, Nova Scotia. They described it to the Rev. John Ambrose, who read an account to the Nova Scotia Institute of Natural Science.

> They now perceived the object to be a large serpent, with a head about the size of a barrel and a body in proportion, and with something like a mane flowing down its neck. It carried its head erect, with a slight inclination forward.
>
> A fisherman belonging to Mill Cove, now came rowing with all his fast decreasing strength to the schooner, and having barely leaped in over the side fainted with terror on the deck.
>
> Wilson thinks the animal was from about seventy to one hundred feet in length.

Also that year is a report from Captain Christmas of a sea serpent that he encountered between Iceland and the Faroes. The captain described the incident to Stephen Cave, MP for Shoreham, who sent an account to Philip Gosse, the famous naturalist, known to be keenly interested in such phenomena.

> He was lying to in a gale of wind, in a frigate of which he had the command, when an immense shoal of porpoises rushed by the ship, as if pursued, and lo and behold a creature with a neck moving like that of a swan, about the thickness of a man's waist, with a head like a horse, raised itself slowly and gracefully from the deep, and seeing the ship it immediately disappeared again, head foremost, like a duck diving. He saw it only for a few seconds; the part above the water seemed about eighteen feet in length. He is a singularly intelligent man, and by no means one to allow his imagination to run away with him.

Here, from a 'singularly intelligent man', is the first clear report of the classic sea serpent with the long snaky neck and small head.

In 1848 occurred one of the most famous and controversial sightings. On 4 October the frigate *Daedalus* arrived in Plymouth from the East Indies, and, soon after its arrival, rumours began to circulate about a sea serpent seen by the

15

captain and crew between the Cape and St Helena. The story appeared in several newspapers including *The Times* of 10 October. The Admiralty wrote to the Captain of the *Daedalus* – Peter M'Quhae – asking for a report of the encounter, and he gave the following reply:

Sir, – in reply to your letter of this day's date, requiring information as to the truth of a statement published in *The Times* newspaper, of a sea serpent of extraordinary dimensions having been seen from Her Majesty's ship *Daedalus,* under my command, on her passage from the East Indies, I have the honour to acquaint you, for the information of my Lords Commissioners of the Admiralty, that at 5 o'clock p.m. on the 6th August last, in latitude 24° 44′ S., and longitude 9° 22′ E., the weather dark and cloudy, wind fresh from the N.W., with a long ocean swell from the S.W., the ship on the port tack heading N.E., by N., something very unusual was seen by Mr Sartoris, midshipman, rapidly approaching the ship from before the beam. The circumstance was immediately reported by him to the officer of the watch, Lieutenant Edgar Drummond, with whom and Mr William Barrett, the master, I was at the time walking the quarter deck. The ship's company were at supper.

On our attention being called to the object it was dis-covered to be an enormous serpent, with head and shoulders kept about four feet constantly above the surface of the sea, and as nearly as we could approximate by comparing it with the length of what our main-topsail yard would show in the water, there was at the very least 60 feet of the animal *à fleur d'eau*, no portion of which was, to our perception, used in propelling the animal through the water, either by vertical or horizontal undulations. It passed rapidly, but so close under our lee quarter, that had it been a man of my acquaintance, I should easily have recognised his features with the naked eye; and it did not, either in approaching the ship or after it had passed our wake, deviate in the slightest degree from its course to the S.W., which it held on at the pace of from 12 to 15 miles an hour, apparently on some determined purpose.

16

The diameter of the serpent was about 15 or 16 inches behind the head, which was, without any doubt, that of a snake, and it was never, during the 20 mins that it continued in sight of our glasses, once below the surface of the water; its colour a dark brown, with yellowish white about the throat. It had no fins, but something like the mane of a horse, or rather a bunch of seaweed, washed about its back. It was seen by the quartermaster, the boatswain's mate, and the man at the wheel, in addition to myself and officers above mentioned.

I am having a drawing of the serpent made from a sketch taken immediately after it was seen, which I hope to have ready for transmission to my Lords Commissioners of the Admiralty by tomorrow's post.

The letter was published in *The Times* on 13 October and caused much excitement. On 28 October the *Illustrated London News* published the pictures that Captain M'Quhae had promised (see plates 3 and 4) Captain M'Quhae's account was confirmed by that of Lieutenant Drummond, which appeared in an article in the *Zoologist*.

One of the people who threw themselves into the resultant controversy was Sir Richard Owen. Sir Richard, though an experienced naturalist, was a very reactionary man (for instance, he totally rejected the theory of evolution) and refused to accept the possibility of a sea serpent. He wrote a letter on the *Daedalus* affair to a friend and part of it was later published in *The Times*. The substance of the letter was that the creature seen by the men of the *Daedalus* was really the Elephant seal (see plate 5) which reaches a length of 20 feet [6 metres], and that the captain and crew had exaggerated the length of the beast by about 40 feet [12 metres]. Owen backed up his argument with much ingenuity but he should not have descended to the level of casting doubt on the reported size to dismiss the sighting. He also maintained that the captain's account had been distorted by a preconceived belief in sea serpents. Owen's letter brought a stinging reply from Captain M'Quhae, who angrily denied exaggerating the creature's length, saying that he and his crew had many years' experience of viewing and estimating the lengths of objects in the water. He also strongly denied having any preconceptions of sea serpents.

Owen was right in thinking that the description was like that of a mammal rather than that of a snake, but the captain had quite honestly reported what he had seen, likening it to a snake, probably the only elongated animal with a small head that he could compare it with. The creature in Captain M'Quhae's picture seems most likely to be the long-necked type of sea serpent. The 'mane' seems quite definitely from the pictures to be fur on the creature's back, rather than long strands on its neck, the latter being a characteristic of a different type of sea serpent.

At this point we should take stock of the situation so far. As the years went by and the reports became more frequent, the believers and the sceptics became more fanatical and antagonistic. The believers were firmly convinced of the existence of just one type of sea serpent – a surviving species of giant reptile from the Mesozoic Era – plesiosaurs being the favourite candidates. This view was partly a result of the contemporary discoveries of the fossil remains of the huge Mesozoic sea reptiles, some of which would seem to make very satisfactory sea serpents. However, as the sceptics rightly pointed out, most of the reported characteristics were mammalian, and they said that those sightings not due to hoaxes and optical illusions were faulty, exaggerated descriptions of known marine mammals. An unbiased person reading the accounts of sea serpents will see that there are several types, and will probably come to the conclusion that most of them are giant mammals unknown to science. Such a conclusion would have offered a compromise and a way out for both camps, but as it was not put forward until many years afterwards the two factions remained totally irreconcilable.

Now let us return to the sightings. In 1856 a sea serpent was seen off the coast of South Africa by the men of the *Princess*. Here is what Captain Tremearne entered in the ship's log:

Tuesday, July 8, 1856. Latitude accurate 34° 56′ S.,
Longitude accurate 18° 14′ E., At one p.m. saw a very

large fish, with a head like a walrus, and twelve fins,
similar to those of a blackfish, but turned the contrary
way. The back was from 20 to 30 feet long; also a great
length of tail. It is not improbable that this monster has
been taken for the great sea serpent. Fired and hit it near
the head with a rifle ball.

This is indeed a bizarre report but there are several
references to similar creatures by early naturalists. Aristotle
wrote of unknown sea creatures with many fins. The third-
century naturalist Aelian, in his book *On the Nature of
Animals,* refers to a 'great sea centipede', centipedes, of
course, having many legs. Guillaume Rondelet, in his
sixteenth-century *L'Histoire entière des poissons,* talks of a
'cetacean centipede' with many feet which 'are as oars with
which it propels itself'. At this point not much can be said
about this type of sea serpent but there are far more detailed
reports of it to come.

In 1860 W. H. Marshall wrote a book called *Four Years in
Burma* in which he described a monster he had seen in the
Indian Ocean.

As the *Nemesis* was proceeding onwards towards our
destination our attention was directed to an alligator of
enormous length, which was swimming along against the
tide (here very strong), at a rate which was perfectly
astonishing. I never beheld such a monster. It passed
within a very short distance from us, its head and nearly
half its body out of the water. I should think that it could
not have been less than five and forty feet long, measured
from the head to the extremity of the tail, and I am
confident it was travelling at the rate of at least, thirty
miles an hour.

One might assume that this was merely a sighting of a
normal member of the crocodile family, its length exaggerated
by the witness. However, there are several reliable reports of
this creature which give a similar length, more than twice
the size of the largest known sea-going crocodile.

The next report is of a more familiar sea serpent, the type

with the mane and big eyes. On 6 May 1863 the mail-packet *Athenian* was on a passage from Tenerife to Bathurst. At about 7 o'clock that morning John Chapple, quartermaster, saw something floating towards the ship. One of the ship's officers wrote a letter about it to a friend, part of which appeared in the *Zoologist* and in the *Illustrated London News*.

> He called the attention of the Rev. Mr Smith and another passenger who were on deck at the time, to it. On nearing the steamer it was discovered to be a large snake about 100 feet long, of a dark brown colour, head and tail out of the water, the body slightly under. On its head was something like a mane or sea-weed.

In 1872 there was a report of a creature resembling a giant eel, from Commander Dyer who saw the creature from HMS *Torch,* off Ghana, on 26 July. 'A large eel-shaped fish with dark brown and light belly, put its head about twenty or thirty feet into the air and came down with a great thwack on the water.'

It seems certain that this creature is a fish, the colouration and rearing action being typical of known species of eel.

All this might seem to be a somewhat bewildering display of strange beasts, but it is possible to categorise the different types of sea serpent, according to their distinguishing features:

1 Having many small humps along the back
2 Showing several big coils above water
3 Having a mane and prominent eyes
4 Having a long neck and small head
5 Having many fins
6 Resembling a huge crocodile
7 Resembling a giant eel

These seem to be the main types of large unknown sea creature. There are two other types which will be described in detail later:

8 Resembling a giant turtle

9 Resembling a giant yellow tadpole

However, there are very few reliable sightings of these two types. The vast majority of the genuine reports fall into these nine categories, and the list of characteristics should help the reader to distinguish the different types in the following pages.

THREE
The Nineteenth Century II

He was at least one thousand yards long, of which about one third appeared on the surface of the water at every stroke of his enormous fan-shaped tail, with which he propelled himself, raising it high above the waves, and arching his back like a land snake or caterpillar. In shape and proportion he much resembled the cobra, being marked by the same knotty and swollen protuberance at the back of the head on the neck. The latter was the thickest part of the serpent. His head was like a bull's in shape, his eyes large and glowing, his ears had circular tips and were level with his eyes, and his head was surrounded by a horny crest, which he erected and depressed at pleasure. He swam with great rapidity and lashed the sea into a foam, like breakers dashed over jagged rocks. The sun shone brightly upon him; and with a good glass I saw his overlapping scales open and shut with every arch of his sinuous back coloured like a rainbow.

The reader, of course, will have recognised this as an obvious hoax. It comes from Mr J. Cobbin, of Durban, who said that he saw the beast from the *Silvery Wave* off South Africa in December 1871. The story of the sea serpent is cluttered with such hoaxes and they have helped to bring the subject into disrepute. The hoaxes are all remarkably similar and can easily be distinguished from the genuine reports. The creatures they describe are always impossibly huge and hybrid, described in excessive detail and in an over-dramatised manner. Most are probably perpetrated in order to gain money and publicity and they naturally need to be sensational to achieve such ends. A hoax might also be intended to ridicule someone, or even specifically to discredit the subject of sea serpents, but whatever its motives it seldom remains undiscovered for long. It seems that there have been about fifty hoaxes in the history of the sea serpent.

Such reports delight the sceptics, but the following cannot be dismissed so contemptuously. The incident is described with obvious restraint and objectivity by the Rev. John Macrae and the Rev. David Twopenny, who sent an account to the journal *Land and Water*.

On the 20th August 1872 we started from Glenelg in a small cutter, the *Leda,* for an excursion to Lochourn. Our party consisted besides ourselves, of two ladies, F., and K., a gentleman, G.B. and a highland lad. [It was later revealed that F., K., and G.B. were the Rev. John Macrae's daughters and grandson.] Our course lay down the Sound of Sleat, which on that side divides the Isle of Skye from the mainland, the average breadth of the channel in that part being two miles. It was calm and sunshiny, not a breath of air, and the sea perfectly smooth.

As we were getting the cutter along with oars we percieved a dark mass about two hundred yards astern of us, to the north. While we were looking at it with our glasses (we had three on board) another similar black lump rose to the left of the first, leaving an interval between; then another and another followed, all in regular order. We did not doubt its being one living creature: It moved slowly across our wake, and disappeared. Presently the first mass, which was evidently the head, reappeared, and was followed by the rising of the other black lumps as before. Sometimes three appeared, sometimes four, five or six, and then sank again. When they rose, the head appeared first, if it had been down, and the lumps rose after it in regular order, beginning always with that next the head, and rising gently; but when they sank, they all sank together rather abruptly, sometimes leaving the head visible.

It gave the impression of a creature crooking up its back
to sun itself. There was no appearance of undulation; when
the lumps sank, other lumps did not rise in the intervals
between them. The greatest number we counted was seven,
making eight with the head . . . The parts were separated
from each other by intervals of about their own length,
the head being rather smaller and flatter than the rest, and
the nose being very slightly visible above the water; but we
did not see the head raised above the surface either this or
the next day, nor could we see the eye. We had no means
of measuring the length with any accuracy; but taking the
distance from the centre of one lump to the centre of the
next to be six feet, and it could scarcely be less, the whole
length of the portion visible, including the intervals submerged, would be forty-five feet.

Presently, as we were watching the creature, it began to
approach us rapidly, causing a great agitation in the sea.
Nearly the whole of the body, if not all of it, had now
disappeared, and the head advanced at a great rate in the
midst of a shower of fine spray, which was evidently raised
in some way by the quick movement of the animal — it
did not appear how — and not by spouting. F. was alarmed
and retreated to the cabin, crying out that the creature was
coming down upon us. When within about a hundred yards
from us it sank and moved away in the direction of Skye,
just under the surface of the water, for we could trace its
course by the waves it raised on the still sea to the distance
of a mile or more. After this it continued at intervals to
show itself, careering about at a distance, as long as we
were in that part of the Sound, the head and a small part
only of the body being visible on the surface; but we did
not again on that day see it so near nor so well as at first.
At one time F. and K. and G.B. saw a fin sticking up at a
little distance back from the head, but neither of us were
then observing.

On our return the next day we were again becalmed on
the north side of the opening of Lochourn, where it is
about three miles wide, the day warm and sunshiny as
before. As we were dragging slowly along in the afternoon
the creature [appeared] again over towards the south side, at

a greater distance than we saw it the first day. It now showed itself in three or four rather long lines and looked considerably longer than it did the day before as nearly as we could compute, it looked at least sixty feet in length. Soon it began careering about, showing but a small part of itself, as on the day before, and appeared to be going up Lochourn.

Later in the afternoon, when we were still becalmed in the mouth of Lochourn, and by using the oars had nearly reached the island of Sandaig, it came rushing past us about a hundred and fifty yards to the south, on its return from Lochourn. It went with great rapidity, its black head only being visible through the clear sea, followed by a long trail of agitated water.

The witnesses on the boat later gave their own descriptions of the incident, and they all agreed on every detail. The creature was seen again in Lochourn on 22 and 23 August by Lord Macdonald and his guests on his steam yacht.

Figure 3   The Leda *sea serpent*

On 8 July 1875 Captain Drevar and the crew of the barque *Pauline,* about twenty miles off the coast of Cape San Roque, watched a titanic fight between a sperm whale and what seemed to be a huge sea serpent. Captain Drevar entered a description in the log, and this was later published.

The weather fine and clear, wind and sea moderate. Observed some black spots on the water, and a whitish pillar, about thirty feet high above them. At the first glance I took all to be breakers as the sea was splashing up fountain-like about them, and the pillar a pinacle rock, bleached with the sun; but the pillar fell with a splash, and a similar one rose. They rose and fell alternately in quick succession, and good glasses showed me it was a monstrous sea serpent coiled twice round a large sperm whale. The head and tail parts, each about thirty feet long, were acting

26

as levers, twisting itself and victim round with great velocity. They sank out of sight about every two minutes, coming to the surface still revolving; and the struggles of the whale and two other whales that were near, frantic with excitement, made the sea in their vicinity like a boiling cauldron; and a loud and confused noise was distinctly heard. This strange occurrence lasted some fifteen minutes, and finished with the tail portion of the whale being elevated straight in the air, then waving backwards and forwards, and lashing the water furiously in the last death struggle, when the body disappeared from view, going down head foremost to the bottom, where no doubt it was gorged at the serpent's leisure; and that monster of monsters may have been many months in a state of coma, digesting the huge mouthful. . . . I think the serpent was about 160 or 170 feet long, and seven or eight feet in girth. It was in colour much like a conger eel; and the head, from the mouth being always open, appeared the largest part of the body.

Captain Drevar saw the animal again five days later:

At seven A.M., July 13, in the same latitude, and some eighty miles east of San Roque I was astonished to see the same or similar monster. It was throwing its head and about 40 feet of its body in a horizontal position out of water as it passed onwards by the stern of the vessel.

It has been suggested that what the captain saw was a giant squid, its tentacles thrown around the whale, but this does not explain the open mouth or the distinctive eel-like colouration. Also, one would expect a squid to show some recognisable feature like its huge eyes, head or body, and the animal seen a few days later was nothing like a squid. It could have been a different creature from that seen by the *Pauline* but the coincidence seems too unlikely. A giant eel seems the nearest approximation to the beast, and would certainly have the strength and flexibility to fight a whale in the manner described. Captain Drevar was subjected to much ridicule from the newspapers, several of which published highly sensational accounts of the incident. This naturally infuriated him and when the ship returned to Liverpool he and his men went before Justice of the Peace T. S. Raffles and swore affidavits as to what they had seen.

In 1875 were two more reports from New England, the first described by the Rev. Arthur Lawrence to the Rev. J. G. Wood, a naturalist seeking reports of sea serpents.

> On the 30th July, 1875, a party of us were on the yacht *Princess,* and while sailing between Swampscott and Egg Rock, we saw a very strange creature. As nearly as we could judge from a distance of about one hundred and fifty yards, its head resembled that of a turtle or snake, black above and white beneath. It raised its head from time to time some six or eight feet out of the water, keeping it out from five to ten seconds at a time. At the back of the neck there was a fin, resembling that of a blackfish, and underneath, some distance below its throat, was a projection which looked as if it might have been the beginning of a pair of fins or flippers like those of a seal. But as to that, we could not be sure, as the creature never raised itself far enough out of the water to enable us to decide. Its head seemed to be about two and a half feet in diameter. Of its length we could not judge, as only its head and neck were visible.

The animal was also seen by several fishermen at the same time and they confirmed the Rev. Lawrence's description. A few days later Captain Garten, of the steamer *Norman,* wrote a letter to a Bridgetown newspaper describing a similar beast he had seen thirty miles south of Swampscott Bay a fortnight earlier.

> The head of the monster was raised at least ten feet above the ocean, but remained stationary only a moment, as it was almost constantly in motion; now diving for a moment, and as suddenly reappearing to the same height. The submarine leviathan was striped black and white, the stripes running lengthways, from the head to the tail. The throat was pure white and the head, which was extremely large,

was full black, from which, just above the lizard-shaped head, protruded an inch or more, a pair of deep black eyes, as large as ordinary saucers. The body was round, like a fish barrel, and the length was more than one hundred feet.

The only report from 1876 is a very strange one and comes from the Indian Ocean. The beast was seen from the *Nestor,* and Captain Webster and Dr Anderson, the ship's surgeon, swore to the account before Donald Spence, acting law secretary to the British Supreme Court in Shanghai.

On September 11, at 10.30 a.m. fifteen miles north-west of North Sand Lighthouse, in the Malacca Straits, the weather being fine and the sea smooth, the captain saw an object which had been pointed out by the third officer as 'a shoal!' Surprised at finding a shoal in such a well known track, I watched the object, and found that it was in motion, keeping up the same speed with the ship, and retaining about the same distance as first seen. The shape of the creature I would compare to that of a gigantic frog. [he seems to mean gigantic tadpole] The head, of a pale yellowish colour was about twenty feet in length, and six feet of the crown were above the water. I tried in vain to make out the eyes and mouth; the mouth may, however, have been below water. The head was immediately connected with the body, without any indication of a neck. The body was about forty-five or fifty feet long, and of an oval shape, perfectly smooth, but there may have been a slight ridge along the spine. The back rose some five feet above the water. An immense tail, fully one hundred and fifty feet in length, rose a few inches above the water. This tail I saw distinctly from its junction with the body to its extremity; it seemed cylindrical, with a very slight taper, and I estimate its diameter at four feet. The body and tail were marked with alternate bands of stripes, black and pale yellow in colour. The stripes were distinct to the very extremity of the tail. I cannot say whether the tail terminated in a fin or not. The creature possessed no fins or paddles so far as we could perceive.

29

The captain later described how the animal had swum round the ship for nearly half-an-hour, giving everyone on board a clear view of it. The account was reported by Richard Proctor in the *Liverpool Echo*. Needless to say, many people tried to explain away the creature, one of the suggestions being that it was a whale shark (see plate 6) whose rows of transverse spots might have looked like stripes when seen from the side. However, the largest whale sharks are no more than 60 feet [18 metres] long, considerably smaller than the *Nestor's* animal. Also, as we shall see, there are other reports of a 'giant tadpole' the details of which rule out this possibility. Proctor himself made the sensible suggestion that the monster was a huge unknown member of the skate family.

On 30 July 1877 in the middle of the Atlantic, John Hart, helmsman of the *Sacramento*, saw a huge animal swimming in the water. He called the captain, W. H. Nelson to see the creature, and later drew a picture of the beast which was published in the *Australian Sketcher* along with his description:

> This is a correct sketch of the sea-serpent seen by me while on board the ship *Sacramento*, on her passage from New York to Melbourne, I being at the wheel at the time. It had the body of a very large snake; its length appeared to me to be about fifty feet or sixty feet. Its head was like an alligator's, with a pair of flippers about ten feet from its head. The colour was of a reddish brown. At the time seen it was lying perfectly still, with its head raised about three feet above the surface of the sea, and as it got thirty or forty feet astern, it dropped its head.

This creature is similar to that seen by the *Nemesis* in the Indian Ocean, and on seeing the picture (see plate 7) one immediately thinks of a crocodile. However, the only sea-going crocodile is the Double Crested Crocodile from the East Indies and Pacific, which has been seen 500 miles [800 kilometres] from land, but the *Sacramento* sighting is 10,000 miles [16,000 kilometres] from its normal habitat. Also, this crocodile is only 20 feet [6 metres] long – half the length of the beast seen by John Hart. Remembering that in the

Mesozoic Era there were several species of sea-going crocodiles, one wonders whether such creatures could not have survived, undetected like the coelacanth, until the present day and this aspect of the story will be discussed in a later part of the book.

This year the sea serpent reappeared at Gloucester Bay. It was seen by the marine painter George S. Wasson and his friend B. L. Fernald who were out in Wasson's yacht the *Gulnare*. They gave an account to the Rev. J. G. Wood.

The day was hazy, with light breeze from the southeast. When we were, as I should judge, about two miles from the mouth of Gloucester harbor, the monster came to the surface about the eighth of a mile to leeward of us. I was looking that way, and saw him appear, but Mr Fernald did not, the first time. He immediately noticed the surging noise made and turning, exclaimed 'What ledge was that which broke?' This is exactly what the sound most resembled, – a heavy ground swell breaking over a submerged ledge; and the creature itself looked, both in shape and color, more like a ledge covered with kelp than anything else we could think of, though from the extreme roughness of the surface I remember that we both spoke of its being somewhat like a gigantic alligator. The skin was not only rough, but the surface was very uneven, and covered with enormous humps of varying sizes, some being as large as a two-bushel basket. Near one end was a marked depression, which we took to be the neck. In front of this, the head (?) rose out of the water perhaps half as high as the body, but we saw no eyes, mouth, fins, or the slightest indication of a tail. It impressed us above all as being a shapeless creature of enormous bulk. I suppose its extreme height out of the water might have been ten feet, certainly not less; and as it disappeared the water closed in over it with a tremendous roar and surge and spray, many feet into the air. The water for a large space where it had been remained white and seething with foam for some little time. From the way the water closed in over it, and the great commotion caused by its disappearing, we judged of its immense bulk, and we also concluded that it went down perpendicularly. It apparently rose in the same way.

Wasson later stated that the creature was from 40 to 60 feet [12 –18 metres] long, dark brown, and moving at a rate of about six knots. Of the many suggestions as to the identity of the many-humped sea serpent, the most sensible came from the Rev. Wood. He thought that it might be descended from the *Zeuglodon,* an extinct species of ancient whale, and he pointed out several characteristics common to them both. Like all whales, *Zeuglodon* could rise and sink vertically in the water, as did Wasson's beast; it was of a similar length – 60 to 70 feet [18 –21 metres]; its skeletal structure indicates that it could rear the front of its body out of the water as did the sea serpent, and, finally, *Zeuglodon* probably possessed the black-and-white colouration of many whales, also a feature of the sea serpent. This theory still remains the most plausible, and might apply to other types of sea serpent, notably the Scandinavian type. Without going into too much detail at this point, Pastor Bing's drawing of Hans Egede's sea serpent is very similar to reconstructions of *Zeuglodon* (see plate 8).

In 1880 Captain Brocklehurst encountered a strange creature in the North Pacific:

1880, August 11th Sea smooth! Ther. 58. hot sun at noon. Lat. 48. 37 N. Long. 180. crossing from Japan to San Francisco. Sitting alone on poop of steamer *Oceanic* at noon, looking at flying fish, saw a long serpent in water 1 or 2 feet below surface, along side the vessel, thought length 40 feet, circumference 2 to 4 feet, pale yellow colour, dark line on back and on ribs, head a little larger than body, could not see any fins, saw it for 5 or 6 mins and then mentioned it to friends on board.

No one could accuse Captain Brocklehurst of over-dramatising the incident. His laconic report seems to refer to the same type of creature as that seen from the *Nestor* in 1876.

On 31 May 1882 the steamer *Katie* was returning from New York to Newcastle, and about 8 miles [12.8 kilometres] from the Hebrides a long dark object was seen in the water. Captain Weisz first assumed it to be the hull of a wrecked ship but as they drew closer he realised his error, as he described in the following account which appeared in the *Newcastle Weekly Chronicle*:

First we took it for a wreck, as the highest end resembled the bow and forepart of a ship, and the remaining bumpy part resembled the broken waist of a ship filled with water. As we got nearer we saw with a glass on the left of the visible object, the water moving in a manner, as if the object extended there under the water, and this motion was of the same length as the part of the object visible above the surface. Therefore we took care, not to steer too near, lest the screw should be damaged by some floating piece of the wreck. But on getting nearer we observed that the object was not a wreck, and, if we had not known with certainty that on these coasts there are no shallows, we should have taken this dark connected row of bumps for rocks. When however, we changed our course obliquely from the object, which lay quite still all the time, to our astonishment there rose, about eighty feet from the visible end, a fin about ten feet in height, which moved a few times, while the body gradually sank below the surface. In consequence of this the most elevated end rose, and could distinctly be made out as the tail of a fish of immense dimensions.

The length of the visible part of the creature which had not the slightest resemblance to a whale, measured, according to our estimation, about 150 feet, the bumps, which were from three to four feet in height, and about six or seven feet distant from each other, were smaller on the tail end than on the head end, which withdrew from our observation. At our arrival at Newcastle, I learned that some days before some fishermen of Lewis had observed the same or similar animal.

Captain Weisz had Andrew Schultz, the animal painter, do an engraving to his instructions.

In the autumn of 1883 the whaler *Hope On* encountered a sea serpent near the Las Perlas Archipelago, south of Panama. The creature was seen by Captain Seymour and the entire crew, and an account appeared in the *Newcastle Weekly Chronicle*:

A head like that of a horse rose from the water and then dived. The creature was seen by all the boat's crew. Captain Seymour describes the animal as almost twenty feet in length, with a handsome horse-like head, with two unicorn-shaped horns protruding from it. The creature had four legs or double-jointed fins, a brownish hide, profusely speckled with large black spots, and a tail which appeared to be divided into parts.

This somewhat bizarre description seems to refer to the long-necked type of sea serpent with four large paddles. Horns are mentioned in several other accounts of this creature, but they are probably fleshy protuberances rather than true horns. The description of the tail might well refer to the two hind flippers joined together in the middle like those of a sea-lion.

In 1885 a giant yellow sea serpent appeared off Morewood Bay, Umhlali, South Africa. A description was found in an unidentified newspaper cutting discovered in the archives of Dr Oudemans, a biologist who was patiently amassing a wealth of information on sea serpents.

According to the account furnished by those who witnessed the sight, the monster appeared to proceed at the rate of about eight miles an hour, occasionally plunging into the water, making a noise as if a sea was breaking heavily on an open shore and causing a foam to extend for about twenty yards on either side of it. It appeared to be about fifteen or twenty feet out of the water, and its whole length was computed at not less than ninety or a hundred feet. Fins like immense oars were then striking the water on either side. It had a large stripe down the body, the remaining portion being of a dirty yellowish colour.

The value of this report would be debatable if it was unique, but it is remarkably similar to the descriptions of the *Nestor*'s 'giant tadpole' and the *Oceanic*'s monster.

In 1889 there was a report from the Mediterranean. The witness, a captain, preferred anonymity, not usually a good sign, but his report, which he sent to the London journal *Answers,* is sober and convincing:

> About three years ago when going up the Mediterranean, and when half-way between Gibraltar and Algiers, and twenty miles from land, I saw, as I thought at first, two masts or wreckage of some ship standing out of the water, but presently seeing that they were moving, and evidently something alive, I naturally was very intent in watching them. They gradually drew nearer until they got within half a mile or so of me.
>
> I saw then that they were large snakes or sea serpents. They kept up on a parallel line with us for fully half an hour (ship going 8½ knots). They then struck off in a different direction.
>
> I had a good view of them with the naked eye, but with the telescope I could see them as distinctly as if they had been on the ship's deck. One was a little longer than the other. I judged the longer to be not less than 30 feet, the other four or five feet shorter. The longer carried its head from four or five feet out of the water, the shorter one not so high by a foot. Their heads in shape were not unlike a greyhound's head without ears.

These creatures seem to be the long-necked type of sea serpent.

So far very few scientists had had the courage to write about sea serpents, the subject being riddled with hoaxes, contradictions and bitter scientific wrangles. However, in 1892 a tremendously important work was published. It was called *The Great Sea Serpent,* ran to 592 pages and was written by Antoon Cornellis Oudemans, one of the greatest scientists to study the sea serpents.

Antoon Cornellis Oudemans was born in Batavia on 12 November 1858, into a family which had a history of academic achievement. From an early age he was interested in natural history and in 1878, at the age of 20, he began to study biology at the University of Utrecht. His doctoral thesis was on the nemertean worms and appeared in 1885, but some years earlier he had published an article in the *Album de Natur* about sea serpents and their probable nature.

He knew relatively little about the subject at the time, having read very few reports of eye witness sightings, and he laboured, like many others, under the belief that there was only one kind of sea serpent. Nevertheless, he quickly discounted the possibility of reptilian sea serpents, though the Rev. J. G. Wood had already advanced the theory that sea serpents could be descended from the *Zeuglodon,* an extinct species of the ancient whales or *Archaeoceti.*

At this time some scientists thought that the whales should be classed with the pinnipeds – the group that comprises the seals, sea-lions and walruses – with *Zeuglodon* as a transitional group or maybe even a common ancestor. Oudemans himself subscribed to this view, but soon went even further, classing the *Zeuglodon* firmly amongst the pinnipeds. He proposed that the ancestor of this conglomerate group was a long-tailed protopinniped which had also branched off by itself and become the group that was the sea serpents.

We know today that this grouping of the whales and pinnipeds together is incorrect, and that *Zeuglodon* was definitely a whale. However, the idea that some types of sea serpent might be related to the pinnipeds and others to the *Zeuglodon* and ancient whales is still valid.

Oudemans undertook his work with great determination, finally arriving at a creature which was like a huge long-necked seal (see figure 4). He proposed to retain the name of *Megophias* or 'big snake' given to the New England sea serpent by the naturalist Rafinesque, who thought that it was a reptile.

Oudemans's theory was a great step forward but it had many flaws, the greatest being that he believed that there was only one type of sea serpent. It seems that there are several types, one of which is almost certainly a reptile like a giant crocodile, and another being some sort of giant eel. Oudemans became very dogmatic in his views and this distorted his treatment of the subject. He rejected many sightings that did not conform to his views and accepted many dubious ones that did. Nevertheless, his book, though suffering much criticism and attacked unmercifully by some, did shake the scientific world and won much support for the existence of the sea serpent.

Oudemans retired at 65 in 1923 and set to work on his vast treatise on the acarids — the mites and ticks — which had also been a lifelong interest. He continued adding to his files on sea serpents, and wrote several articles and treatises on the Loch Ness Monster, which became famous in the 1930s. He died in 1943 at the age of 85, leaving a vast amount of invaluable material on the subject of sea serpents.

Figure 4 Megophias, *after A. C. Oudemans*

In 1893 a sea serpent was encounterd by the steamer *Umfuli*, off Mauritania. Captain Cringle gave this account:

When we first saw it, I estimated that it would be about 400 yards away. It was rushing through the water at great speed, and was throwing water from its breast as a vessel throws water from her bows. I saw full 15ft of its head and neck on three separate occasions. . . . The body was all the time visible. The base or body, from which the neck sprang, was much thicker than the neck itself, and I should not therefore, call it a serpent. Had it been breezy enough to ruffle the water, or hazy, I should have had some doubt about the creature; but the sea being so perfectly smooth, I had not the slightlest doubt in my mind as to its being a sea monster. . . . This thing, whatever it was, was in sight for over an hour. In fact we did not lose sight of it until darkness came on.

The unfortunate captain suffered so much ridicule that he later wrote:

I have been so ridiculed about the thing that I have many times wished that anybody else had seen that sea monster rather than me. I have been told that it was a string of

37

porpoises, that it was an island of seaweed, and I do not know what besides. But if an island of seaweed can travel at the rate of fourteen knots, or if a string of porpoises can stand 15 ft out of the water, then I give in, and confess myself deceived. Such, however, could not be.

Figure 5 The Umfuli *sea serpent, after Captain Cringle*

In the years 1897 and 1898 there was a remarkable series of sightings from the French gunboats along the coast of Indo-China. The first sightings were by Lieutenant Lagrésille, commander of the *Avalanche,* in 1897, though he did not describe it until a year later when he saw the beast again. The account appeared in the *Courier d' Haiphong.*

> In the month of July last the *Avalanche* saw for the first time, off Along Bay, two animals of weird shape and large dimensions; their length was reckoned at about 65 feet and their diameter at 6 to 10 feet. The feature of these animals was that their body was not rigid like those of the known cetaceans, but made undulatory movements similar to a snake's but in a vertical direction. A revolving gun was loaded and fired at 600 yards, at slightly too short range. They immediately dived, breathing loudly and leaving a wash on the surface like breakers. They did not reappear, but we thought we saw their heads, which we judged to be of small dimensions.
> On 15 February of this year, when crossing the bay of Fai-tsi-long, I saw similar animals again. I at once gave chase and had the revolving guns loaded. Several shots were fired at one of them, at ranges of between 300 and 400 yards, and at least two shots reached them without seeming to do them the least harm, the shells bursting on the surface. I also tried to reach them with the bow of

the ship, but their speed was greater than that of the
Avalanche. Each time, however, that this animal came
into shallow water it turned back, which enabled me to
gain upon it and confirm its great size. It frequently
emerged, and one always noticed its undulatory move-
ments. Each emergence was preceded by a jet of water, or
rather water vapour made by a loud breath, unlike the
ordinary blowers which inhale water and blow it out to a
certain height.

The colour of this animal was grey with several black
fins. . . .

On 25 February that year Lagrésille was invited to a
reception given by Admiral de la Bodéllière in honour of
Paul Doumer, the governor general of Indo-China. On this
occasion Lagrésille described his encounter with the sea
serpent to a very sceptical audience, but his story was soon
borne out. Next day Lagrésille invited Commander Joannet
and several officers from the gunboat *Bayard* to a meal on
the *Avalanche* while it cruised through the Fai-tsi-long
archipelago. In the middle of dinner one of the crew shouted
for everyone to come on deck, for there, swimming along a
few hundred yards away, were two of the monsters that
Lagrésille had described. Lagrésille reported that:

We gave chase to one of them for thirty-five minutes, and
at one particular moment we saw it clearly about 200
yards on the beam, floating horizontally. It had three
undulations without a break, which ended with the
appearance of its head, which much resembled a seal's, but
almost double the size. We could not see whether it had a
neck, joining it to the body, of relatively much greater
dimensions: this was the only time we saw the undulations
appear without a break. Until then we might have thought
that what we took for them were humps appearing in
succession; but from the testimony of all the witnesses
doubt is no longer permissible, for, before they appeared,
we saw the animal emerging by the same amount all along
its length. Two of the officers present possessed a camera:
they ought to have been able to use it then, but they were

so surprised by what they saw, that when they thought of aiming their cameras the animal dived, only to appear much further away in much less clear conditions, unfavourable to taking a photograph.

To sum up, the animals seen by the *Avalanche* are not known. Their length is about 65 feet (minimum), their colour grey and black, their head resembles that of a seal, and their body is subject to undulations that are sometimes very marked: finally their back is covered with a sort of saw-teeth which removes any resemblance to known cetaceans; like the latter they reveal their presence by blowing noisily. . . .

Naturally the visitors were very excited and reported the encounter to Admiral de la Bodéllière, who not only apologised to Lagrésille for doubting him, but immediately made plans for capturing one of the beasts by driving it into shallow water. However, his plans were thwarted by the crisis at Kwangtung.

The myths and legends of the Eastern seas parallel the modern reports of sea serpents in a striking manner. A Vietnamese collection of such myths, the *Chich-Quai*, talks of a huge, twisting sea serpent with many fins or legs in the waters of the Gulf of Tongking. Like Aelian and Rondelet, it uses the simile of the centipede, a creature which, in addition to its many legs, has a segmented body. A similar beast is the Lord-of-the-Sea of Malagasy legend. Dr Petit, from the Paris Museum, collected details of it from the Malagasy natives, which he included in his book *L'Industrie des Pêches à Madagascar,* published in 1930:

The Lord-of-the-Sea appears rarely, but he shows himself, whenever the time may be, by always moving against the wind. He is 70 to 80 feet long, and his wide flat body is covered with hard plates, rather like the bony armour on the back of a crocodile, but bigger. The tail is like a shrimp's tail with its terminal flap. The mouth is ventral, the animal must turn on its back to attack. A sort of hood which the animal may raise and lower at will protects the eyes which look forwards but are placed well to the side.

The head is luminous and shines lights as it comes to the surface. It moves in vertical undulations.

Some Malagasies say the animal has no legs. Others say it has front flippers like a whale's.

Of course, these folk-tales and native descriptions do not prove anything, but they do confirm, in almost every respect, the details given in modern reports of this creature. However, there is more solid evidence than this. In 1883 there had been a report of a strange carcase washed ashore in Hongay in Along Bay. One of the witnesses was a native, Tran Van Con, who described the remains, many years later in 1921, to Dr Krempf, of the Oceanographic and Fisheries Service of Indo-China. He said that the putrefying body, from which the head was missing, was some 60 feet [18 metres] long and segmented, each segment having a pair of large lateral fins. The colour was dark brown above and yellowish underneath. This description is consistent with both the native legends and the French reports.

With all this information it is possible to suggest a family to which this creature could belong.

The French reports describe it as undulating vertically and spouting like a whale, and some of the Malagasies said that it had a pair of fore-flippers like those of a whale. So it seems very likely that the many-finned sea serpent is a member of the whale family.

Furthermore, the bony segmented armour, as described by the Malagasies and Tran Van Con, is also believed to have been a feature of the *Archaeoceti,* or ancient whales, one species of which was the *Zeuglodon.*

The many lateral fins, which are the basis of the traditional description of a 'centipede' are certainly not true skeletal fins, but probably fleshy excrescences, which might be supported by projections in the animal's bony dermic armour.

The Rev. J. G. Wood had already proposed that the many-humped sea serpent could be a descendant of the *Archaeoceti,* and it seems likely that the many-finned sea serpent is also related to this group.

By the end of the nineteenth century sea serpents had achieved a certain amount of respectability. They were even mentioned in the *Encyclopedia Britannica* in 1886, being given a sceptical but fairly open-minded treatment, the writer admitting that some reports could not be explained by known phenomena. More scientists began to take the subject seriously, particularly after the publication of Dr Oudemans's *The Great Sea Serpent* in 1892, a significant year for sea serpents as it also brought the death of their bitterest enemy – Sir Richard Owen.

FOUR
The Twentieth Century

One of the first sightings of the twentieth century was in 1901, though it did not come to light until 1947, when one of the witnesses, Charles Seibert, sent a description to the *Saturday Evening Post.* The letter was one of many sent in response to an article in the paper by Ivan T. Sanderson, called 'Don't Scoff At Sea Serpents!' In May 1901 the steamer *Grangense* was on passage from New York to Belem, and one fine morning the officer of the watch shouted 'My God, look there!'

> Looking as directed we saw some sort of an amphibian, grayish brown in color. The forward part, which was all we could see, was similar to the monster illustrated in the *Post*; however its neck was not so thick or long. Its head was a trifle longer, more like a crocodile's. When it opened its mouth, we could see rows of regular teeth, maybe four to six inches long. It appeared to be playing on the surface, and would swirl in circles, bending its neck until it looked towards its tail, if it had one. It would gambol for maybe half a minute, then dive. This it did three times. We asked the captain if he was going to log the encounter. His reply was, 'No fear. They will say we were all drunk, and I'll thank you mister, not to mention it to our agents at Para or Manaus.

This seems to be a giant crocodilian, like the animal seen from the *Sacramento.*

In 1903 there was an obvious hoax. It comes from Joseph Grey, second officer of the steamer *Tresco,* which he said encountered a fearful monster south of Cape Hatteras. Needless to say, it terrified the entire crew.

> There was something unspeakably loathsome about the head, which was five feet long from nose to upper extremity. Such a head I never saw on any denizen of the sea. Underneath the jaw there appeared to be a sort of pouch, or drooping skin. The nose, like a snout upturned, was somewhat recurved. . . . I can remember no nostrils or blowholes. The lower jaw was prognathous, and the lower lip was half projecting, half pendulous. Presently I noticed something dripping from the ugly lower jaw. Watching, I saw that it was saliva, of a dirty drab colour. . . . While it displayed no teeth, it did posses very long and formidable molars like a walrus's tusks. . . . Its eyes were also of a reddish colour. . . . They were elongated vertically. They carried in their dull depths a sombre, baleful glow, as if within them was concentrated all the fierce, menacing spirit that raged in the huge bulk behind.

After frightening everybody on board, the creature turned around and swam away – rather an anticlimax.

In the years 1903 and 1904 there were more sightings from Indo-China. The first report was from the *Charles Hardouin* on a passage from Nantes to Hong Kong in the winter of 1903. A typhoon forced the ship to shelter in Tourane Bay, Vietnam, and the helmsman saw a dark mass in the water.

> 15 to 20 yards from the ship a double mass appeared, the length of each part must have been about 25 feet and the distance between them about 18. The bulk of each coil could be compared to that of a big half-hogshead barrel; a spiky crest gave the coils a quite singular appearance.
>
> It all undulated like a snake in motion, and its speed was markedly greater than that of the ship, which was then doing 9 knots so far as I recall. The colour was of a dirty black. A few seconds later the animal dived horizontally, churning the water violently.

44

A few months later, on 12 February 1904, a sea serpent was again encountered in Along Bay, this time by Lieutenant Péron of the gunboat *Château-Renault*. Péron was making soundings that morning from a steam launch, when

I saw, not very far ahead, a grey mass shaped like a turtle's back, which we reckoned to be more than 12 feet across; almost at once it disappeared. I supposed it was a sperm-whale. The launch still having way on her, we came near where it had surfaced, and I saw that there was a big patch of oil on the water.

I still remained stopped, and am glad I did; soon after-wards we heard the water churning to the west, and we saw, almost touching the nearby shore a little south of Chandelier Rock, two huge coils which I supposed must belong to a monstrous eel at least 3 feet in diameter. I saw to my great surprise that the skin of this beast and the rocks on the shore were the same colour; dark grey with patches of dirty yellow. From the distance that I was the skin seemed smooth and even. It appeared briefly, the two coils disappeared with a repetition of the noise we had already heard. . . . I got the impression that the animal was just awash and moving by vertical undulations.

Péron told Lieutenant L'Eost of the *Décidée* about his experience, and found that he too had seen the animal. As time went by it became apparent that many people had seen the monster of Along Bay, which, translated from the dialect, is significantly, Dragon Bay. Commander E. Plessis, who served under L'Eost, wrote that 'in the staff of the Naval Division in Indo-China, all the officers firmly believed in its existence'.

Many sceptics, including Sir Richard Owen, had complained that witnesses of alleged sea serpents were always ignorant of zoological principles, and so could not be relied upon to report accurately what they had seen. Presumably the next report answers such criticism, for it was made by two naturalists, Fellows of the Zoological Society, M. J. Nicoll and E. G. B. Meade-Waldo. They both gave reports to the Zoological Society and Nicoll also described it at length in his book *Three Voyages of a Naturalist,* published in 1908.

> At 10.15 a.m. on Thursday, 7th December, 1905, when in latitude 7° 14′ S. longitude 34° 25′ W., and in a depth from 322 –1,340 fathoms, Mr E. G. B. Meade-Waldo and I saw a most extraordinary creature about 100 yards from the ship moving in the same direction but very much slower than we were going. At first all we could see was a dorsal fin, about 4 feet long, sticking up about 2 feet from the water; this fin was a brownish-black colour and much resembled a gigantic piece of ribbon-seaweed. Below the water we could distinctly see a very large brownish-black patch, but could not make out the shape of the creature. Every now and then the fin entirely disappeared below water. Suddenly an eel-like neck, about 6 feet long and of the thickness of a man's thigh, having a head shaped like that of a turtle, appeared in front of the fin. This head and neck, which were of the same colour above as the fin, but of silvery-white below, lashed up the water with a curious wriggling movement. After this it was so far astern of us we could make out nothing else.

A significant point was made by Meade-Waldo, who said: 'As we drew ahead we could see it swing its neck from side to side. . . .' The colour, shape, and horizontally undulating neck all suggest that this animal was a giant eel. The naturalists' sketch supports this view, showing that there was no distinct junction at the head and neck, this being a fish-like characteristic. The long neck is really an elongated body.

Figure 6   The Valhalla *sea serpent, after M. J. Nicoll and E. G. B. Meade-Waldo*

A year later there was a Dutch report from the steamer

Java, 600 miles off Somalia. Judging from the entry in the log by one of the officers, J. Vollewens, it was of the giant crocodile type.

In 10° 7.5′ N. latitude, 59° 23′ E. longitude on 15 October 1906 seaman J. A. Spruijt, saw the head of a sea-monster raised some 6 feet out of the water, by his reckoning at 200 yards; it was shaped like a cayman, brown in colour, with a smooth skin, and was followed directly by the beginning of a body of the same colour.

The next three reports refer to the long-necked sea sepent, a type which seems to be on the ascendant in the twentieth century.

In 1907 a sea serpent was reported by Sir Arthur Rostron, then Chief Officer of the *Campania,* which encountered the animal off Cork, Ireland, on 26 April. It appeared as a dark object sticking up some 9 feet [2.7 metres] out of the water only 50 yards [45 metres] from the ship. Rostron, staggered, described it thus:

So strange an animal was it that I remember crying out: 'It's alive!' One had heard such yarns about these monsters and cocked a speculative eye at the teller, that I wished as never before that I had a camera in my hands. Failing that, I did the next best thing and on the white 'dodger board' in front of me I made sketches of the animal, full face and profile, for the thing was turning its head from side to side for all the world as a bird will on a lawn between its pecks.

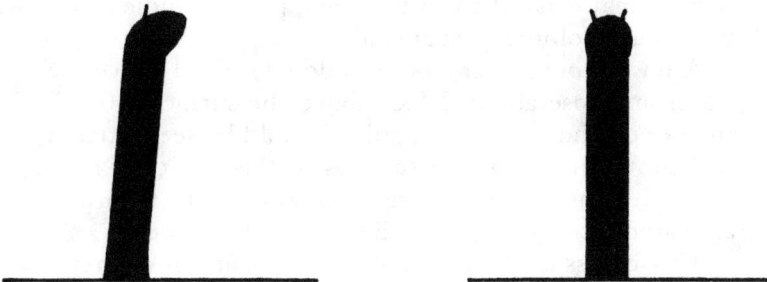

Figure 7   The Campania *sea serpent, after Sir Arthur Rostron*

In 1910 came a sighting from the North Atlantic, by
F. W. Eep, third officer of the steamer *Potsdam*. An account
appeared in the Dutch journal *Nederlandsche Zeewezen*:

> From close to, it seemed to us to be shaped like a gigantic
> snake, 120 to 130 feet long, and about 2 feet in diameter.
> It was moving very fast. From time to time the head was
> raised almost perpendicularly out of the water, up to a
> height of 8 or 10 feet; it remained in this position for some
> time and then disappeared again. These two movements
> went with a considerable splashing of water that rose to
> about 20 feet, while the tail stirred up the water no less
> violently (the tail was flat and wide in shape with a forked
> end). One could also see one bend of the body. The colour
> was dark grey above and white below, which was very
> clearly marked on the head. The animal was watched for
> about three minutes.

This is one of the few reports of the long-necked sea
serpent which mentions a tail, describing it as forked, as did
Captain Seymour of the *Hope On*. This 'tail' could be two
hind flippers like those of a seal or sea-lion.

A year later a similar creature was seen in the same vicinity
by J. A. Liebau, of the Dutch steamer *Amsfeldijk*. He made
the following entry in the log:

> On Saturday, 19th August, at half past one in the after-
> noon an animal was observed which was very probably a
> sea serpent. Our attention was suddenly drawn by some-
> thing hitting the sea fairly violently; about 60 yards to
> port a great mass of foam was seen, in the middle of which
> was a dark coloured sea animal.
>
> A few seconds later a body suddenly lifted above the
> water and rose about 8 feet above the surface; 30 feet
> further on the back of the animal could be seen. After it
> had shown itself for ten seconds in this position, it fell
> back into the water, hitting it violently, and then dis-
> appeared into the depths and was seen no more.
>
> This colossus was about 2 feet 6 inches in diameter
> (that is in the part out of the water). A large proportion of

the part that emerged seemed to belong to the head and sank progressively with the body. The diameter of the head seemed to our eyes to be a little greater that that of the rest of the visible part. The back was dark in colour, while the ventral part was much lighter. Because it appeared so suddenly, and at a considerable distance, we could not observe it more closely.

In 1912 we have two reports which undoubtedly refer to the giant eel type of sea serpent, the first coming from A. F. Rodger, third mate of the *Queen Eleanor* which was travelling past Cape Matapan on the Greek coast. Rodger described the incident many years later in response to a BBC broadcast on sea serpents in 1961. Rodger had seen the beast swimming parallel to the ship and described it as about 30 feet [9 metres] long, 18 inches [45 centimetres] in diameter, of a mottled colour, and like a huge eel. Later in the year Captain Ruser and the first officer of the *Kaiserin Augustus Viktoria* saw a similar creature off the coast of Prawle Point, South Devon. It was smaller than the *Queen Eleanor*'s sea serpent, being about 20 feet [6 metres] long, 18 inches [45 centimetres] in diameter, and like an eel in colour, being blue-grey on top with a whitish belly.

In the year 1913 there was an amazing report of what seems to have been a young sea serpent out of the water! The account comes from Hartwell Condor, a Tasmanian State mining engineer, who was prospecting the little-known territory between Maquane and Fort Davey on the west coast of Tasmania. One day, two of Condor's men reported seeing a strange animal in the area and Condor reported the incident to Mr Wallace, the Tasmanian Secretary of Mines, who gave an account to the press:

The animal was seen by Oscar Davies, foreman prospector, and his mate (W. Harris), who are working under myself. . . . I have known both of them for a considerable number of years, and can guarantee absolutely their sobriety, intelligence and accuracy. They were walking along the coast on April 20, just before sundown on a calm day, with small waves rolling in and breaking on the shore, when at a distance of about half-a-mile, they noticed a dark object under the dunes which surprised them by showing signs of movement. They advanced towards it, and finally came within gunshot. When about forty yards off it rose suddenly and rushed down into the sea. After getting out about thirty yards it stopped and turned around, showing only the head above five seconds, and then withdrew under the water and disappeared.

The characteristics are summarised as follows: It was fifteen feet long. It had a very small head, only about the size of the head of a kangaroo dog. It had a thick arched neck, passing gradually into the barrel of the body. It had no definite tail and no fins. It was furred, the coat in appearance resembling that of a horse of chestnut colour, well groomed and shining. It had four distinct legs. It travelled by bounding – that is, by arching its back and gathering up its body so that the footprints of the forefeet were level with those of the hind feet. It made definite footprints. These showed circular impressions with a diameter (measured) of 9 inches, and the marks of claws, about 7 inches long, extending outwards from the body. There was no evidence for or against webbing. The creature travelled very fast. A kangaroo dog followed it hard in its course to the water and in that distance gained about 30 feet. When first disturbed it reared up and turned on its hind legs. Its height, standing on the four legs, would be from 3 ft 6 in. to 4 ft.

Both men are quite familar with seals and so-called sea leopards that occur on this coast. They had also seen before and subsequently pictures of sea lions and other marine animals, and can find no resemblance to the animal that they saw.

This animal sounds very similar to some members of the seal family, but there are several differences. Sea-lions, fur seals and walruses, which can turn their hind legs to the front and bound along, are not indigenous to Tasmania. There are two species of sea-lion found on the south and west coasts of Australia, and they might stray to Tasmania, but they are only 8 feet [2.4 metres] long, have short necks and could not make footprints as large as those found by Condor's men. It seems very likely that this animal was a young specimen of the long-necked type of sea serpent, a creature similar to Oudemans's *Megophias,* but without a long tail.

With the commencement of the 1914 war, shipping was to face far deadlier under-water hazards than sea serpents. However, there are at least seven reports from the war years, one account being given by the survivors of HMS *Hilary,* which, two days before being sunk by a U-boat, had fired on and apparently killed an unfortunate many-humped creature off the coast of Iceland. There are also two clear U-boat reports of giant crocodilian creatures, the first being in 1915, from Commander Freiherr von Forstner of the U 28 (see plate 9):

On 30th July our U 28 torpedoed the British steamer *Iberian* (5,223 tons) carrying a rich cargo in the North Atlantic. The steamer, which was about 600 feet long, sank quickly, the bow sticking almost vertically into the air, towards the bottom, a thousand fathoms or more below. When the steamer had been gone for about 25 seconds, there was a violent explosion at a depth which it was clearly impossible for us to know, but which we can reckon, without risking being far out, at about 500 fathoms. A little later pieces of wreckage, and among them a gigantic sea animal, writhing and struggling wildly, were shot out of the water to a height of 60 to 100 feet.

At that moment I had with me in the conning tower my officers of the watch, the chief engineer, the navigator and the helmsman. Simultaneously we all drew one another's attention to this wonder of the seas. As it was not in Brockhaus nor in Brehm we were, alas, unable to identify it. We did not have the time to take a photograph, for the animal sank out of sight after 10 or 15 seconds. . . . It was about 60 feet long, and was like a crocodile in shape and had four limbs with powerful webbed feet and a long tail tapering to a point.

That the animal should have been driven up from a great depth seemed to me very understandable. After the explosion, however it was caused, the 'underwater crocodile,' as we called it, was shot upwards by the

51

terrific pressure until it leapt out of the water gasping and terrified.

Actually it is unlikely that the wreck had sunk to 500 fathoms in only 25 seconds, and the animal was probably fairly close to the surface when the blast hurled it into the air. Forstner's account appeared in the *Deutsche Allgemeine Zeitung* in 1933 and shortly after its publication another U-boat commander. Werner Lowisch, came forward with a description of a similar beast he had encountered in the North Sea in 1918. On the evening of 28 July he and a crew member of the U 109 had seen a huge animal with 'a long head, jaws like a crocodile's and legs with very definite feet'.

In 1919 J. Mackintosh Bell, a Scottish lawyer, took a fishing holiday in the Orkneys, during which he saw a sea serpent frequently spoken of by the local fishermen. On 5 August he was out with his friends and several local men lifting lobster creels between Brims Ness and Tor Ness, and at about 9.30 that morning one of the fishermen drew everyone's attention to a creature which had quietly surfaced a short distance away. Bell gave an account and a little sketch:

I looked and sure enough about 25 –30 yards from the boat a long neck as thick as an elephant's fore leg, all rough-looking like an elephant's hide, was sticking up. On top of this was the head which was much smaller in proportion, but of the same colour. The head was like that of a dog, coming sharp to the nose. The eye was black and small, and the whiskers were black. The neck, I should say, stuck about 5 –6 feet, possibly more, out of the water.

It disappeared, and as was its custom swam alongside the boat about 10 feet down. We all saw it plainly, my friends remarking that they had seen it many times swimming just the same way after it had shown itself on the surface. My friends told me that they had seen it the year before just about the same place. It was a common occurrence, so they said.

That year (1919) was the last of several years in which they saw it annually. It did not show itself again for two or three years, and then it was only seen once. As to its body, it was, seen below the water, dark brown, getting slightly lighter as it got to the outer edge, then at the edges appeared to be almost grey. It had two paddles or fins on its sides and two at its stern. My friends thought it would weigh 2 or 3 tons, some thinking 4 to 6.

Bell later said that the creature was about 20 feet [6 metres] long, about 10 to 11 feet [3 –3.5 metres] round the body, and with a neck about 8 feet [2.4 metres] long. He also made a rough sketch.

Figure 8 The Orkneys sea serpent, after J. M. Bell

Both this and the Tasmanian report show that the long-necked sea serpent is tail-less, and has a pair of hind flippers like those of a seal or sea-lion.

The warm waters off California seem to be a favourite haunt of sea serpents, west coast residents being very proud of their local monsters – 'Bobo' of Cape San Martin, the 'Old Man' of Monterey Bay, and, most well-documented of all, the San Clemente Monster. These beasts all seem to be the maned sea serpents with the big eyes, and a good description of the San Clemente Monster comes from Ralph Bandini, secretary of the Tuna Big Game Fishing Club, who in September 1920 was out fishing near San Clemente with his friend Smith Warren. At about 8 o'clock in the morning:

All of a sudden I saw something dark and big heave up. I seized my glasses. What I saw brought me up straight!
 A great columnar neck and head, I guess that is what it was, lifting a good 10 feet. It must have been five or six feet thick. Something that appeared to be a kind of mane

of coarse hair, almost like a fine seaweed, hung dankly. But the eyes – those were what held me! Huge, seemingly bulging, round – at least a foot in diameter!

We swung towards it. . . . Then even as I watched through the glasses, the thing sank. There was no swirl, no fuss, . . . just a leisurely, majestic sinking – and it disappeared, about a quarter of a mile away.

Bandini, who described the incident in his book *Tight Lines,* saw the beast twice again in those waters, but not so close as on that occasion. There have been many other witnesses, though, one being George Farnsworth, President of the Tuna Club, who gives us this description:

Its eyes were 12 inches in diameter, not set on the side like an ordinary fish but more central. It had a big mane of hair about two feet long. We were within a hundred feet of it before it went down. This was no sea elephant. It was some kind of mammal, for it could not have been standing so long unless it was.

J. Charles Davis II, author of many fishing works, interviewed as many witnesses as he could find and said: 'It was almost as though a recording had been made and each man played the same record . . . these men were all interviewed separately and none of them knew that I had talked to anyone else about the San Clemente Monster!'

In 1923 there was a sighting from the Thames Estuary, in an area known as the Black Deep, which had been closed to shipping for eight years when the beast was seen. The witnesses were the captain and crew of HMS *Kellett* which was surveying the area at about 9 o'clock on a summer morning. Captain Haselfoot and Commander Southern saw a long neck rise out of the water about 200 yards [180 metres] from the ship. It rose to a height of 7 feet [2 metres] and then submerged, to reappear soon after, again rearing itself out of the water for a few seconds. Captain Haselfoot drew a rough sketch of the beast.

1   Oarfish washed ashore at Newport Beach, California, 1901

2   A few moments after the critical identification as a Coelacanth, on Captain Hunt's vessel at Pamanzi, Comores, 29 December 1952. This was the second coelacanth to be caught by Europeans, the first being trawled up off Madagascar in 1939. Professor J. L. B. Smith is seated at the creature's head

3   The *Daedalus* sea serpent, 1848

4   The *Daedalus* sea serpent, 1848

5   Elephant seal

6 Whale shark, length about 60 feet [18 metres]

7 The *Sacramento* sea serpent, 1877

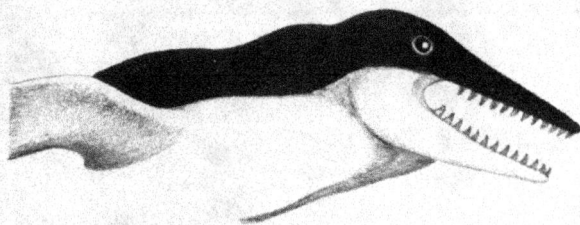

8 *Zeuglodon*

9 The U28 sea serpent, 1915 after the sketch by Dr Richard Hennig

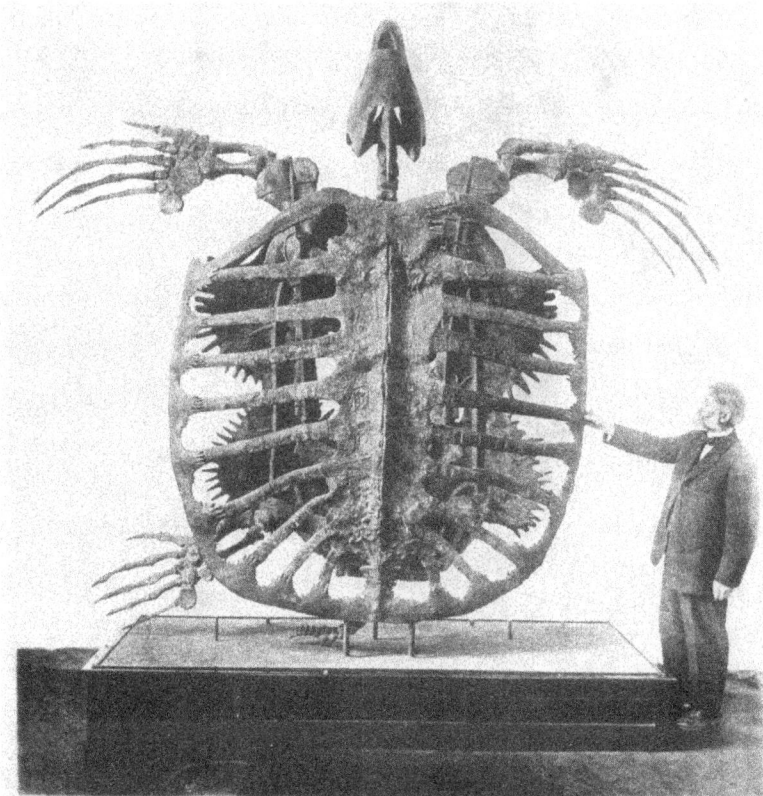

10 *Archelon*

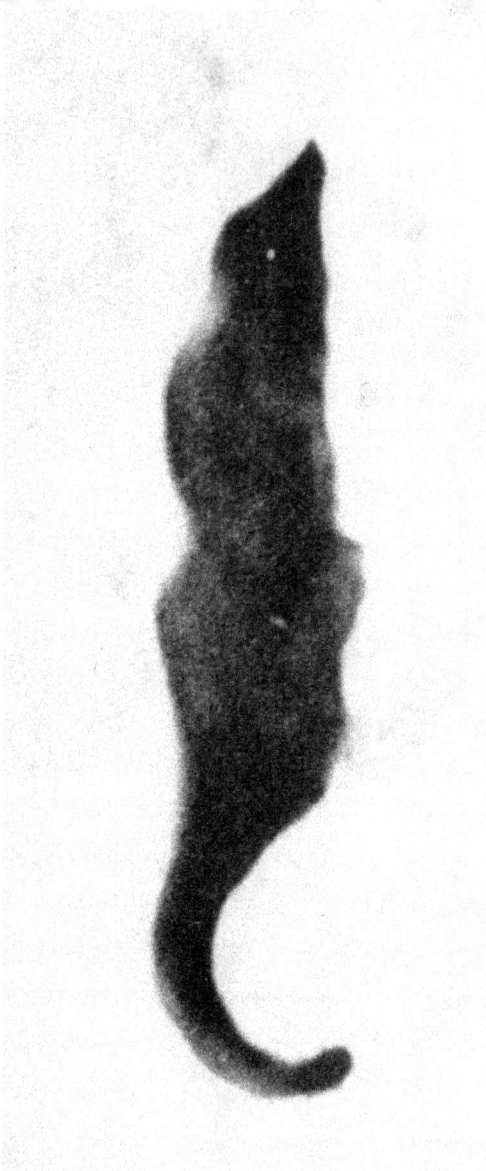

11 Mary F's photograph of the Falmouth Bay sea serpent

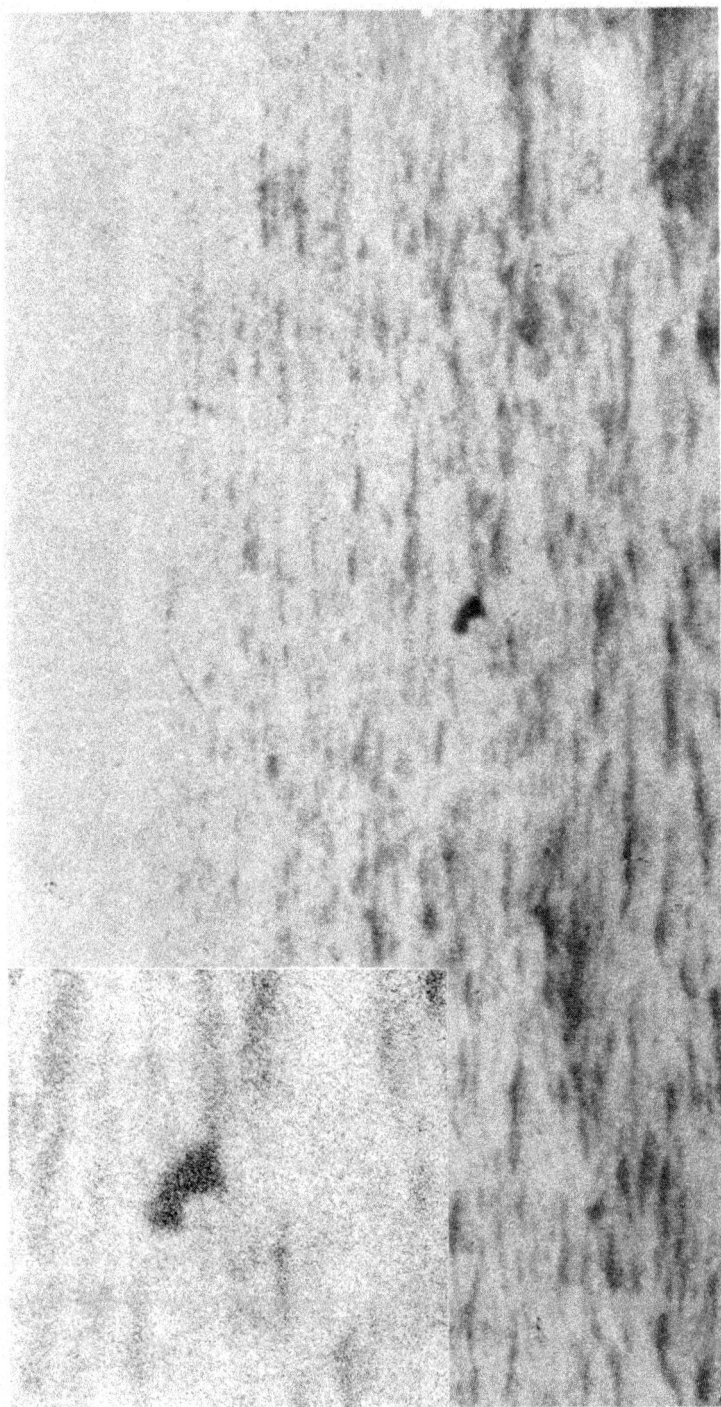

12 and 13   The Falmouth Bay sea serpent, photograph by Tony Shiels

14 The Querqueville carcase, 1934

15 A giant squid stranded on the coast of Yorkshire in 1925. Giant squids are known to attain a length of 60 feet (18 metres)

Figure 9   The Kellett *sea serpent, after Captain Haselfoot*

In 1934 there was another terrestrial sighting, this time from the prosaic background of Filey, Yorkshire. The account appeared in the *Daily Telegraph* on 1 March.

Mr Wilkinson Herbert, a Filey coastguard, says he saw the thing on shore last night; a dark moonless night. He was walking along Filey Brig, a long spur of rocks running out to sea, when: 'Suddenly I heard a growling like a dozen dogs ahead, walking nearer I switched on my torch, and was confronted by a huge neck, six yards ahead of me, rearing up 8 feet high!

The head was a startling sight – huge tortoise eyes, like saucers, glaring at me, the creature's mouth was a foot wide and its neck would be a yard round.

The monster appeared as startled as I was. Shining my torch along the ground, I saw a body about 30 feet long. I thought "This is no place for me" and from a distance I threw stones at the creature. It moved away growling fiercely, and I saw the huge black body had two humps on it and four short legs with huge flappers on them. I could not see any tail. It moved quickly, rolling from side to side, and went into the sea. From the cliff top I looked down and saw two eyes like torchlights shining out to sea 300 yards away.'

This account refers to the long-necked type of sea serpent, the physical description being virtually the same as that of the animal seen ashore in Tasmania in 1913. The Tasmanian report refers to the creature bounding, arching its back, the Filey report says that the beast moved with a rolling motion. These descriptions could both describe the clumsy gait of a member of the seal family out of the water, and it seems probable that this type of sea serpent is related to the pinnipeds.

Most of the sea serpents described so far fall quite easily into different categories, but occasionally there is an exception, the creature described seeming rather ambiguous. The following is such a report, described in a letter to Tim Dinsdale in 1972, from Mr A. C. Enkel from Essex.

The year was 1936, and the month August when on a touring holiday we drew our caravan to a parking site at Mundesely on the Norfolk coast.

The party included a Mr and Mrs Savage, my wife Marjorie and myself. After having an evening meal Leslie (Savage) suggested we had a final stroll on the beach, while our wives were tidying up. Off we went down the cliffs on to the beach. All of a sudden Leslie said, 'Alec look out there! what do you think it is?' Being quite a distance out to sea, and the evening closing in it was three or four seconds before I caught sight of it, but there it was, the outline plain to see. There were the five curved humps, and the long neck, with a head pointing forward at right angles to the neck, like the head of a large snake, travelling at a terrific speed, and going south-east diagonally from us.

Mr Enkel also said that the humps did not move or change shape, and that the colour was dark brown, almost black. He also made a sketch (see figure 10).

The humps seem too big, and too few in number, to be those of the American many-humped sea serpent. It does not seem to be the Scandinavian type either, because of the colour, the length of the neck, and the fact that the humps did not undulate as a flexible spine would. Also the humps are too sharp to bear any relation to a spinal column. I think the most important features are the long neck with a small head and the 'terrific speed'. We have seen that the long necked type of sea serpent seems to be related to the pinnipeds, a group which can attain very high speed in water. When travelling at these speeds their fat-covered bodies can show several big humps. These humps are turbulence waves in the fat, caused by the surface friction of the water. So, Mr Enkel's sea serpent seems to be of the long-necked type.

Figure 10   The Mundesely sea serpent, after Mr A. C. Enkel

In 1937 there was a report from Scotland, from the Pentland Skerries – a small group of islands between John o' Groats and the Orkneys. The account, from Mr John R. Brown appeared in the *Orcadian*.

Mr Scot was speaking last night about a monster that had been seen about Fair Isle. To tell the truth I never believed much in monsters myself, but I saw something today resembling nothing I have ever seen before.

It was about noon when we were working down at the landing at the East End that on chancing to look out to sea I noticed the sea breaking white as on a submerged rock. As I knew there were no rocks in that particular spot, I watched for a little and presently a great object rose up out of the water – anything from 20 to 30 feet and at an angle of about 45°. It was round-shaped and there appeared

57

to be a head on it, but as it was about half a mile from the shore I could not be sure.

I called the attention of the other two men but unfortunately before they got their eyes on the spot it had disappeared again, though both of them saw the foam it made. We watched for a considerable time but it never appeared again.

Although distance prevented Mr Brown from discerning details of the creature's head and neck, it seems likely to have been a long-necked type.

In 1938 a sea serpent appeared off the coast of Southwold in Suffolk, details of which featured in the *Daily Mirror* and *Daily Mail*. On the morning of 21 October Ernest Watson and William Herrington went out in their boat to lay nets near the South Barnard buoy. While returning to land they were startled by a huge animal which thrust out a long neck from the water about 40 yards [36 metres] away. It then shot off at a speed of some 30 knots and eventually dived amidst a swirling wash. They reckoned it to be about 60 feet [18 metres] in length and dark grey.

There have been many sensational stories of sea serpents sinking ships, but in 1947 we have a well-documented report of an encounter in which the sea serpent was the victim. On 30 December, the liner *Santa Clara* was sailing through a calm sea off North Carolina, when the third officer, John Axelson, drew the attention of the chief mate, William Humphreys, and navigation officer, John Rigney, to a snake-like head which reared up some 30 feet [9 metres] off the starboard bow. The captain, John Fordan, made a detailed statement to the press:

the three watched it unbelievingly as in a moment's time it came abeam of the bridge where they stood, and was then left astern. The creature's head appeared to be about 2½' across, 2' thick and 5' long. The cylindrically shaped body was about 3' thick, and the neck was 1½' in diameter. As the monster came abeam of the bridge it was observed that the water around it, over an area of 30 or 40 feet square, was stained red. The visible part of the body was about 35′ long. It was assumed that the colour of the water was due to the creature's blood and that the stem of the ship had cut the monster in two, but as there was no observer on the other side of the vessel there was no way of estimating what length of body might have been left on that side.

From the time the monster was first sighted until it disappeared in the distance astern it was thrashing about as though in agony. The monster's skin was dark brown, slick and smooth. There were no fins, hair or protuberances on the head, neck or visible part of the body.

The dark, smooth skin, and lack of visible fins suggest that the unfortunate creature was a sea serpent of the giant eel type.

Over the years there have been several reports of a sea serpent off the shores of British Columbia. The reports refer to the maned type of sea serpent with the big eyes, and a fairly typical description comes from George W. Saggers, from Vancouver Island, who saw the beast in 1947 while out fishing.

On my port side, about 150 feet away, was a head and neck raised about four feet above the water, with two jet black eyes about three inches across and protruding from the head like a couple of buns, staring at me.

It just didn't look real. I've never seen anything like it. The head seemed to be the same size as the neck, about eighteen inches through and of a mottled color of grey and light brown. . . .

After it looked at me for one full minute, it turned its head straight away from me, showing the back of its head and its neck. It appeared to have some sort of a mane, which seemed like bundles of warts rather than hair. It looked something like a mattress would, if split down the middle allowing rolls of cotton batting to protrude. The color of the mane was dark brown.

About the same year a similar beast was seen off the Gower Peninsula, Wales, the witness being Mr A. G. Thompson of Swansea, who described the creature in his book *Gower Journey,* published in 1950. He first thought that the object he saw from a cliff top was a log, but then:

> Suddenly one end moved and it became plain that a head like that of a horse with a mane was standing out of the water and watching something on the rocks at the foot of the cliff. What a thrill!! After staring for what seemed minutes the monster appeared to be satisfied and dived with what looked like two distinct undulations of the hind portion. What an uncanny feeling!

In 1956 the crew of the cargo steamer *Rhapsody* reported seeing a huge turtle with a white shell south of Nova Scotia, an area in which a similar beast had been reported in 1883. The *Rhapsody*'s monster was 45 feet [13.5 metres] long with 15-foot [4.5 metres] flippers. Now giant turtles have been reported as such just four times in the history of the sea serpents, hardly enough on which to base an acceptance, but we do know that giant turtles once existed. The largest living species is the leathery turtle, with a maximum length of about 9 feet [2.7 metres], but during the Cretaceous period, which ended about 70 million years ago, lived a species of turtle which attained lengths of 20 to 25 feet [6 to 7.5 metres] – possibly more. It was of the species known as *Archelon* (see plate 10) and its fossil remains have been found in Kansas. Such turtles could have survived in the seas, as did their smaller relatives, and there have been references to giant turtles by various early naturalists. Aelian, in the third century, writes of turtles in the Indian Ocean with shells 24 feet [7.3 metres] across, which were used as the roofs of small dwellings. In the twelfth century Al Edrisi writes of turtles 30 feet [9 metres] long inhabiting the waters off Ceylon. Of course, all this is not proof, and there have been very few sightings of giant turtles but we should not close our minds to the possibility of such creatures existing in the ocean today.

In June 1961 Mr O. D. Rasmussen, of Tonbridge, Kent, wrote to the *Daily Telegraph* describing a sea serpent seen by himself, his family and the crew and passengers of the SS *Taiyuen,* south of the Philippines.

The creature was dark skinned, with a head similar in proportion to a snake's, and a tapering neck thickening as it neared the water by about half as much again as the part immediately behind the head.

The neck disappeared below water level, but two humps followed, evenly spaced by the water in between the three visible parts. These were followed by a barely visible 'wake', stretching for possibly the length of a cricket pitch.

This creature swam parallel with us for about half an hour and then veered half-left away from us to the west, completely disappearing in a similar period. Inasmuch as the *Taiyuen* was steaming about ten knots it could be said that the creature maintained this speed as well.

Unfortunately, Mr Rasmussen did not give the date of the occurrence, but he did provide an excellent sketch.

Figure 11 The Taiyuen *sea serpent, after O. D. Rasmussen*

The next report comes from a Mrs Lilian Lowe of Harborne, Birmingham, who described it in a letter to Tim Dinsdale. The incident occurred on 21 June 1965 on the west coast of Scotland.

Three of us, my husband, my cousin and myself were standing on the end of Mingany Pier, Kilchoan, Ardnamurchan, looking out to sea, which was mirrorlike with not a ripple on the surface. My husband was looking through binoculars (Taylor Hobson ex-army x 6), at the old ruined Mingany Castle.

I saw what I thought to be a seal appear above the water, about 100 yards offshore. Then, another hump appeared, directly behind it and a few feet away. As it moved I came to the conclusion that the two humps belonged to one

61

object. I said 'What's that?' My husband immediately sighted the creature but was silent. He said afterwards he was too amazed to speak. He could see a huge shape about 40 feet long beneath the water, and after a few moments said 'a submarine I think'. He then noticed what seemed to be legs or flippers paddling at the side of the body, creating a turbulence beneath the water. My cousin and I could only see the two humps moving steadily along and waited for a decision as to the identity of the creature, but all my husband could say was that he had never seen anything like it in his life. The two humps were very solid and dark and shiny, and the skin seemed to be like hide.

I was anxious to see it through binoculars . . . but just as I had it in view the creature submerged.

I must state that my husband has exceptionally keen eye-sight and has seen basking sharks off the Cornish coast and is convinced the creature was something he had never before encountered.

This creature seems to be one of the long-necked sea serpents, a type which seems to have a fat-covered body, two humps of which may show above water.

In October 1966 Mr George Ashton, from Sheffield, was on holiday with his wife at Chapel St Leonards near Skegness. The couple were walking along the beach when they saw a sea serpent less than 100 yards [90 metres] offshore, an account of which appeared in the *Skegness Standard*:

It had a head like a serpent and six or seven pointed humps trailing behind it. At first I thought it was a log but it was travelling at about 8 m.p.h. and going parallel with the shore. We watched it for some time coming from the direction of Chapel Point until it disappeared out of sight towards Ingoldmells.

I just didn't believe in these things and tried to convince myself it was a flight of birds just above the water. I even thought of a miniature submarine but after watching it for some time I knew it couldn't be.

The most recent sightings come from Cornwall, a land of

many legends of strange creatures, one of which is a long-necked monster inhabiting Falmouth Bay. The locals called it 'Morgawr' meaning 'Sea Giant'. There have been vague, isolated reports of such a creature in the area throughout the twentieth century, but during the past few years there has been a series of clear accounts, details of which appeared in the local paper, the *Falmouth Packet*.

On a sunny September evening in 1975, Mrs Scott and Mr Riley saw a huge creature off Pendennis Point. They described it as having a small head with two stumpy horns, and a long neck with what looked like coarse hair or bristles on it. As they watched, the creature dived for a few seconds, and then reappeared, clutching what looked like an eel in its jaws.

In January 1976 Mr Duncan Viner, a dental technician from Truro, saw something swimming along a few hundred yards off Rosemullion Head. At first all he could see was a dark hump, which he thought was the back of a whale, but then a long neck reared up out of the water. Mr Viner estimated the creature's length to be between 30 and 40 feet [9 –12 metres].

There were two more sightings that month, the first from Miss Amelia Johnson, who was walking near Rosemullion Head, when she saw a large creature come to the surface in Falmouth Bay. She said that it had two humps and resembled 'a sort of prehistoric dinosaur thing, with a long neck the length of a lamp post'. Tony 'Doc' Shiels, a keen investigator of such phenomena, drew a sketch of the creature to Miss Johnson's instructions.

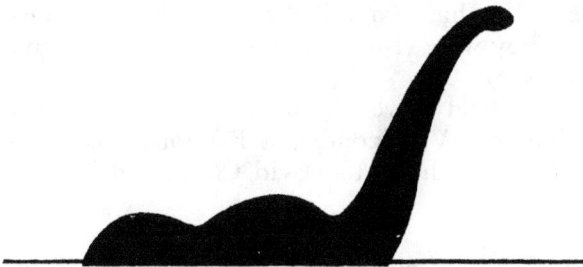

Figure 12   The Falmouth Bay sea serpent, after Miss Amelia Johnson

Also in January was a report from Mr Gerald Bennet of Seworgan who saw a strange creature swimming at the mouth of the Helford River one afternoon. He said that the part above water was 'about twelve feet in length with an elongated neck'.

Towards the end of January a strange carcase was washed ashore at Durgan Beach. It was found by Mrs Payne of Falmouth, and apparently baffled everyone who saw it. Unfortunately it was washed back into the sea before it could be officially identified.

In March the *Falmouth Packet* published a photograph of Morgawr, taken by a lady who called herself Mary F (see plate 11). She said that she had seen the monster off Trefusis Point, and described it as at least 18 feet [5.5 metres] long, with a humped back, long neck and small head, and of a blackish-brown colour. The photograph is consistent with all the eye witness accounts, and looks genuine enough, but Mary F did not send the negatives, and would not reveal her full name or her address. All efforts to contact her have failed. Her reticence is perhaps understandable when we recall how eye witnesses have been ridiculed, but it is unfortunate that the first photograph of a sea serpent should not be completely above suspicion.

In May there was another report, from Tony Rogers and John Chambers, two London bankers on holiday in Falmouth, who gave an account to the *Falmouth Packet*. They were fishing from the rocks of Parson's Beach at the mouth of the Helford, when: 'Suddenly, something rose out of the water about 150 or 200 yards away. It was greeny-grey in colour and appeared to have large humps. Another smaller one also appeared. They were visible for about ten seconds and looked straight at us.'

During the heat wave of August 1976 there was a report from Mr George Vinnicombe, a Falmouth fisherman, who described his encounter to David Clarke, editor of *Cornish Life* magazine.

We were fishing over wartime wrecks in the channel. It was a beautiful calm, clear day. I looked over the starboard side and saw this thing in the water. I thought it was a boat upside down. We went over to investigate and it looked like the back of a dead whale but with three humps and about 18 to 20 feet long. The body was black but a lighter colour under the water. Then suddenly this head came out of the water about three feet from the body. It just looked at us and my mate and I just looked at one another. He said 'What the hell have we got here?' Then the head vanished and the body sank away. I've been fishing for 40 years and it's the first time I've seen anything like that.

In November David Clarke himself saw 'Morgawr', at the mouth of the Helford. He was accompanied by Tony 'Doc' Shiels, who claims to be able to make telepathic contact with sea serpents! Clarke writes:

After discussing Morgawr with Doc Shiels, he agreed to my taking some photos of him standing by the Helford River 'invoking' the monster by magical means! Early in the morning of Wednesday November 17th last year we drove to the village of Mawnan and clambered down the cliffs onto the rocky beach beneath the Church. I duly took pictures of Doc waving his stick at the waves and a few more of the river as fishing boats left the Helford on a rising tide. Doc also took some colour photos of areas where Morgawr had previously been seen. While I was waiting for him, trying to keep warm by throwing stones for my dog to chase, Doc drew my attention to an object half way across the river – a small dark head poking out of the water. We both stood on large rocks for a better view and I attached a telephoto lens to my camera. The object slowly moved nearer and I could see that it was definitely a head, probably a seal. It came within seventy or eighty feet and started to move very slowly up and down river in a zig-zag pattern. It was only when I saw it side-on that I observed that the greenish black head was supported on a long arched neck, more slender than that of a seal. In the wave troughs at least 4 or 5 feet of the neck were visible. There was a slow movement of water stretching back behind the head and neck for about ten feet, and at one point a gently-rounded shiny black body broke the surface.

65

(Doc later said that he had earlier seen two humps.) The head was rounded with a 'blunt' nose and on the top of the head were two small rounded 'buds'.

Doc and I were both busily shouting to one another as we took photos and I must admit to feeling rather afraid as the creature surged back and forth. It had obviously seen us.

At this point my dog, demanding more stones to be thrown, began to bark. The head of the creature turned to us and its mouth opened as it slowly sank and vanished in a swirl of water. We stood for another half an hour looking for more signs, but nothing else appeared.

Unfortunately the winding mechanism of Clarke's camera had slipped repeatedly, so all the negatives were double exposed. However, Shiel's photographs, developed by Boots, were unspoilt, but the creature is at such a distance that details cannot be distinguished. A great enlargement of the pictures (see plates 12 and 13) show a small head on a neck of which most is submerged. As evidence they are interesting, but inconclusive, though Clarke vouches for the fact that they are of the creature that he saw.

David Clarke had always been a sceptic regarding the existence of sea serpents. He is still sceptical, but admits that now he is not so certain of his views.

FIVE
A Classification

We have now considered in detail about a quarter of the 400 reliable accounts which refer to sea serpents. There have also been about 200 mistakes, hoaxes, and dubious sightings, most of which have been excluded from this book for the purpose of clarity. It now remains to classify the reliable reports, depending on their characteristics, and to suggest what groups of animals the unknown creatures have evolved from or are related to. Probably the only scientist to have undertaken this task completely objectively is Dr Bernard Heuvalmans from Holland, and much of this chapter follows upon his conclusions. The sightings are listed on pages 112–31, each with its probable identity.

There seem to be seven main groups of large unknown sea creatures. I think we can rule out the possibility of any of them being invertebrates: they are far larger than all known invertebrates (with the possible exception of the giant squid) and show too many advanced characteristics. Obviously birds can be ruled out, so this leaves the other main vertebrate groups:

Mammals
Reptiles
Fishes
Amphibians

The first five types of sea serpent to be described all seem to be mammalian, their most important characteristic being bodies that undulate vertically, this feature, among vertebrates, being almost exclusively confined to mammals.

1 The Waterhorse (71 probable sightings)

Distinguishing features

> long mane on neck
> very large eyes
> bristles on face and around lips
> neck of medium length
> vertical undulations

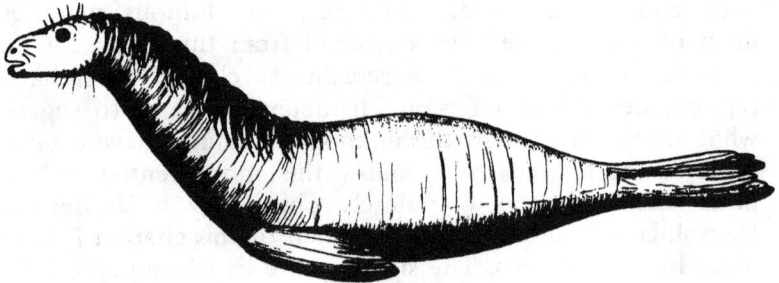

Figure 13   The Waterhorse

The Waterhorse has a head resembling that of a horse or camel, with a distinctive mane on the neck. The eyes are enormous and seem to be black in colour, some reports suggesting phosphorescence, and may show different hues according to the light that they reflect. The mouth is wide and seems to have thick lips, often surrounded by bristles. The tail has been described in some reports as straight and in others as jagged. This suggests that the tail is really two hind flippers like a seal's or sea-lion's, which appear differently according to the position from which they are viewed. The skin appears smooth, which suggests naked flesh, or, more likely, short, close fur like that of seals. The mane is always reddish. It seems likely that there is a pair of fore-flippers. The length is somewhere between 40 and 100 feet [12 –30 metres].

The huge eyes are probably the result of a twilight existence at about 50 to 100 fathoms, from which the animal occasionally surfaces. Apart from the Indian Ocean and Polar seas, the Waterhorse has been seen all over the world, but seems to prefer coastal waters in warm regions, being rarely seen in deep oceans.

The mane may be hair or long filaments of flesh. The Hairy Frog from North West Africa has such filaments on the hind portions of its body and they seem to be a respiratory aid, absorbing oxygen directly from the water. The filaments assume a tangled clotted look when the frog is out of water, and this is how the mane of the Waterhorse is often described. However, such a feature would be very unusual in a mammal.

The large, black eyes, the nose whiskers, and the smooth hide all suggest that the Waterhorse belongs among the pinnipeds – the group that comprises the seals, walruses, and sea-lions.

2 The Scandinavian Giant Otter (29 probable sightings)

Distinguishing features

> shows large coils of its body above water
> moves with vertical undulations
> has a long body
> grey in colour
> small head

The head is small and elongated. The eyes are small and not often mentioned in reports. The neck is slender and of medium length and the tail is long and pointed. The spine is very flexible, often showing six coils above water. Two pairs of webbed feet are seen when the animal rolls or leaps. In the 1750s there was a brief report of such a creature being caught by fishermen at Sundmoer, Norway, and they too said that it had two pairs of limbs. The skin seems rough and wrinkled and of a light, greyish colour. Its length is between 60 and 100 feet [18 –30 metres], but may seem to be more, as the creature makes a long wake, similar to the curves in its body, as it swims with vertical undulations. The animal resembles a huge otter but is almost certainly not related to the otters.

Figure 14 The Scandinavian Giant Otter

This creature normally inhabits cold, northern waters, such as those of Scandinavia and Greenland. It seems likely that the creature swims into warmer waters to breed or give birth.

There have been very few sightings of this creature since the early nineteenth century, suggesting that it is in decline, or maybe even extinct. It is difficult to suggest a family to which this beast could belong. It could hardly be a pinniped for the tail is much too long. The long flexible spine is very like that of the *Zeuglodon,* the best known of the ancient whales of *Archaeoceti.* However, the *Zeuglodon* had no external hind legs, so if the Scandinavian Giant Otter was related to this group it would have had to precede the *Zeuglodon,* possibly even being the ancestral *Archaeocetus.*

3 The Multi-humped (62 probable sightings)

Distinguishing features

   many small humps along back
   moves with vertical undulations

whale-like colouration
oval head

Figure 15 The Multi-humped

The head is oval with a broad snout, and connected by a short neck to a body which shows many small humps along the back. Some reports mention a small fin on the neck or shoulder, and this could be a feature of older specimens or the males of the species. The tail is horizontal and bilobate, the animal undulating in a vertical plane. It has a single pair of fins which are seen when the animal rears the front of its body out of the water. The skin is generally described as smooth, but sometimes witnesses report large lumps or scales on the hide. These could be bony dermic plaques set in the hide. A few mammals possess such plaques, notably the armadillo, in which they form a complete coat of armour, and it is thought that they were also a feature of the *Archaeoceti*. The back is dark and the underside white, a whale-like colouration. Often there are two white stripes on the neck. The length is somewhere between 50 and 100 feet [15 –30 metres].

The Multi-humped may reach speeds of 35 knots. The humps could be fatty lumps or hydrostatic sacs connected to the larynx and inflated at will. If so they might serve as air reserves for long dives, or to lighten the mass of the animal. They would also act as a stabilising influence.

Most sightings of this creature are from the East Coast of the USA, particularly Massachusetts, and it seems to like the warm waters of the Gulf Stream. Sightings become rarer as time goes on, suggesting that the animal may be in decline.

The Multi-humped would seem to be related to the

Archaeoceti. To support this view there is the whale-like colouration, the horizontal bilobate tail, the lack of external hind legs and the possibility of bony plaques in the skin. Also it is believed that the skeletal structure of some members of the *Archaeoceti* permitted them to rear the front portions of their bodies out of the water, as the Multi-humped has been seen to do.

4 The Long-necked Seal (94 probable sightings)

Distinguishing features

long neck
small seal-like head
bulky body lacking distinct tail
four large flippers
vertical undulations

This creature seems to be covered in thick rolls of fat, the appearance varying somewhat according to the displacement of this fat, showing one, two or three big humps. The head is small, resembling that of a dog or seal, and apparently lengthening as the animal grows older. The eyes are small and there are often two small horns mentioned by observers. These horns are probably fleshy protuberances and may be an aid to breathing or to prevent bubbles from obscuring the animal's vision as it exhales underwater. The neck is long and flexible. There are two pairs of flippers, sometimes seen through clear water from above, and occasionally when the animal has been seen ashore. There seems to be no distinct tail, but the hind flippers may resemble a bilobate tail, or, when held together as sometimes seals do, like a fish tail. The skin looks smooth when wet and seen from a distance, but closer observation reveals it to be wrinkled and rough, sometimes showing what looks like coarse fur. It is dark on top, sometimes mottled, and lighter underneath. It seems to be between 30 and 70 feet [9–21 metres] long.

The animal can swim very quickly, attaining speeds of 35 knots, suggesting that it is a predator which chases fish.

Sometimes it has been seen to leave a greasy wake on the water.

It is found all over the world except the polar seas, and the correlation between sightings and climate indicate that it likes warm but not hot regions.

Figure 16 The Long-necked Seal

This creature seems very likely to be a pinniped. The webbed feet or flippers, the absence of tail, and in a few sightings its movement on land – bounding like a sea-lion – point to this conclusion. In addition there is the greasy wake, also a characteristic of pinnipeds.

A Classification

5 The Multi-finned (26 probable sightings)

Distinguishing features

many lateral fins
appearance of segmented armour
vertical undulations
spouts like a whale
dorsal crest

Figure 17 The Multi-finned

The most characteristic feature of this animal is the row of fins which run along the sides of the beast. These seem to be fleshy excrescences rather than true fins and they point forward, almost certainly being used to stabilise the creature. The head is small, with a wide mouth and prominent eyes, and attached to a short slender neck. The skin is smooth, but apparently set with bony plates which give the creature an armoured aspect. On accasions it has been fired at, such as at Along Bay in 1897 by the gunboat *Avalanche,* and the armour seems to give protection. Some reports speak of dorsal fins. These could be a prominent dorsal crest or the lateral fins briefly glimpsed as the animal rolls on its side. It has a small horizontal tail, is of a mottled colour, and is between 50 and 70 feet [15 –21 metres] long.

The Multi-finned moves by vertical undulations of the

body, apparently being obliged to roll on its side to turn. Nearly all the reports say that it spouts like a whale, the breathing also being audible. It may attain a speed of 10 knots when chased.

The Multi-finned frequents the hottest parts of the world, those with temperatures in the region of 30°C. Twice it has been seen in pairs, once in Along Bay, Indo-China, and once off the coast of Somalia.

It seems likely that this creature is related to the whale family. The smooth skin, horizontal tail, and audible breathing suggest this. The bony dermic armour, fleshy fins, and short thin neck are features of the *Archaeoceti*, the ancient whales. Like the Multi-humped and the Scandinavian Giant Otter, the Multi-finned is probably a descendant of the *Archaeoceti*.

The next group of sea serpents displays reptilian characteristics.

6 The Sea Saurian (9 probable sightings)

Distinguishing features

> general appearance of a crocodile
> long head with tooth-filled jaws
> scales on parts of body
> long muscular tail
> undulates horizontally

Figure 18 The Mosasaur

This animal has a reptilian shape very like that of a crocodile or alligator, but is more than twice the size of the largest

A Classification

known member of this group. The head has prominent eyes and a large, tooth-filled mouth. It has two pairs of flippers or webbed feet and a powerful tail, which it has been seen to lash from side to side, in the water. It is mainly smooth, with scales or warts in places.

It seems to prefer warm waters, i.e. the Indian Ocean, the Pacific and the warmer parts of the Atlantic, often being seen in the deepest seas, thousands of miles from land.

In the Mesozoic Era, which ended about 70 million years ago, there were three reptile groups, all crocodilian in shape, from which this creature could be descended: the Thalatto-suchians, the Kronosaurs, and the Mosasaurs. The Thalatto-suchians were an early form of true crocodile and were well adapted to a marine life. They were up to 50 feet [15 metres] long, with large flippers, and in some species a fish-like tail. The Kronosaurs were sea-going descendants of the Nothosaurs, the group which also gave rise to the Plesiosaurs. They attained lengths of up to 40 feet [12 metres]. The Mosasaurs were perhaps the most advanced of the great sea reptiles. They belong to a more recently evolved group than other marine reptiles and were highly specialised for a marine life. Their vertebrae were constructed in such a way as to allow great lateral movement, probably allowing them to swim by this means alone, without help from their flippers. The bones of their skulls were tremendously reinforced, suggesting that they could dive to great depths. The largest known species were about 40 feet [12 metres] long. It is possible that one of these three reptile groups survived until the present day, and the Mosasaur is the most likely candidate.

The last main group of sea serpents seems to belong among the fishes.

7 **The Giant Eel (25 probable sightings)**

Distinguishing features

   no distinct joint between head and neck
   no limbs
   tapering tail

eel-like colouration
leaps out of water and falls back with a splash

The Giant Eels are a very diverse group, those seen differing
in many ways. The only common features are the smooth
skin, a head which merges straight into the neck, and a long,
tapering tail ending in a point. Some have blunt heads like
the common eel, and some have pointed heads like the
congers and morays. Some seem to have a terminal mouth
and others a ventral one. Some are dark on top, white underneath, and others – particularly the Mediterranean variety –
are a mottled colour. Some reports mention a dorsal fin, soft
and translucent. Pectoral fins are mentioned in some reports
but not others, either because there are none, or because they
are small and held close to the body. The lengths vary from
20 to 100 feet [6 –30 metres].

The Giant Eels are often seen on the surface in dramatic
circumstances, e.g. apparently wounded, writhing in agony,
or fighting with other creatures, such as whales, eels having
tremendously powerful bodies. They are also seen rearing up
out of the water and falling back with a splash, this being a
characteristic of known eels. They seem to be deep water
dwellers, though cosmopolitan, sightings coming from all
over the world, but the mottled variety seems to be exclusively
Mediterranean.

It is possible that some members of this group might be
giant eel-like selachians, rather than true eels. There is some
evidence for this which will be discussed in the next chapter.

The foregoing are the seven main groups of sea serpent.
There are two other types to be described, but the scarcity
of sightings makes them seem rather dubious. They could
be faulty observations of known creatures, but this seems
unlikely.

8 The Giant Tadpole (5 probable sightings)

Distinguishing features

general shape like that of a huge tadpole

77

long, tapering tail ending in a point
yellow with black lateral stripes

This animal resembles a huge tadpole, coloured yellow with black stripes on its sides, and occasionally a black stripe on its spine. The head merges into the body, and the tail is very long and like a whip-lash. The length seems to be between 60 and 200 feet [18 –60 metres].

This creature seems to be confined to the Indian Ocean and the Pacific, usually being seen in summer. It seems to prefer warm conditions.

It is very difficult even to suggest a family to which this creature could belong. Mammals and reptiles seem out of the question. It might be an amphibian, though this is highly unlikely, as there are no known marine amphibians. This is because the skin of amphibians is a highly sensitive organ used in respiration, and it could not function in sea water without major adaptations. The most likely possibility is that it is a fish, possibly one of the selachians, such as a huge unknown species of ray.

9 The Giant Turtle (4 probable sightings)

Distinguishing features

resembles a huge turtle

We can say very little about this creature. The scarcity of sightings makes it difficult to accept. Of course, its existence is possible and it could be a descendant of the *Archelon,* the giant turtle of the Mesozoic Era.

In addition to the above categories I have added two others:

Unclassifiable (11 probable sightings)

This refers to sightings which are so strange as to defy

explanation (assuming them to be genuine reports). One is described in the next chapter.

Undefined Extension (39 probable sightings)

This refers to those sightings which, because of inadequate description, great distance, or poor visibility, could be of either the Long-necked Seal or the Giant Eel.

I am aware that the foregoing classification is subject to criticisms, particularly criticisms based on the behaviour and habits of known creatures. For example, critics of the pinniped theories might say that known seals nearly always come ashore to breed and give birth, and they are of a friendly and curious nature, these features apparently lacking in the Waterhorse and Long-necked Seal. There are many such questions, but I think we should be wary of basing theories as to the *identity* of unknown animals on our knowledge of the *lifestyle* of known ones. Many creatures have adapted in ways that would be inconceivable had we not captured specimens of them, or observed their behaviour in zoos. This chapter is based on the apparent physiology of sea serpents.

Also, I think that, having accepted an eye witness testimony, we should not distort or re-interpret what was said. For example, Maurice Burton, accepting the possibility of a Giant Eel, and believing it to be much more probable than the existence of large unknown mammals, used it to explain the American sightings of many-humped sea serpents. He postulated that a Giant Eel swimming on its side at the surface would show a series of large humps. This is an ingenious theory but it simply does not fit the eye witness descriptions. They said that the humps were solid and static, part of a creature which had a definite neck and head, and which swam with vertical undulations.

Even if the reader does not accept this classification, I hope that he accepts that there are probably several types of sea serpent. But is there any solid evidence for their existence? The next chapter deals with this question.

SIX
Stranded
Specimens

A question frequently asked by sceptics is 'If there are sea serpents why aren't they caught, or their remains washed ashore?' The answer is that there *have* been mysterious creatures netted and washed up and, although most turn out to be known animals, there are several cases where the specimens were almost certainly unknown to science, probably of some of the sea serpents described in this book. Before examining these cases, though, it should be explained how the rotting remains of a known creature can be taken for those of a sea serpent, and to do so it is necessary to examine the anatomy of the basking shark of the genus *Squalus*.

The basking shark is a harmless, plankton-eating fish which inhabits the colder waters of the world. Its maximum size would seem to be about 40 feet [12 metres], but most are considerably smaller. Its name is derived from its lifestyle of drifting lazily through the water letting plankton float into its mouth. The plankton are caught on a bony grille while the water passes out through the gills. Being cartilaginous, like all sharks, skates, and rays, it has very little solid structure except a long backbone which extends into the upper lobe of the tail, and apart from this there is only soft cartilage and flesh. When the creature's carcase decomposes all that is left is the small skull, the backbone, and sometimes the pectoral fins. The gill frames, which in the *Squalus* nearly encircle the neck, fall away with the jaws, and the remains look very like a plesiosaur or similar beast, though an expert examination usually reveals their true nature.

Figure 19 Basking shark. Shaded areas are those which disintegrate rapidly on decaying carcase

Another puzzling characteristic of a decaying *Squalus* is that it possesses what seems to be hair. This 'hair' is in fact fibres of muscle and flesh which break into whiskers as the skin rots away.

Until the latter half of the eighteenth century many naturalists still described the natural world in a rather credulous, exaggerated way, so it is often hard to distinguish the truth in some of their stranger reports. One of the more accurate naturalists was Bishop Erik Ludvigsen Pontoppidan of Norway, and in his book *The Natural History of Norway,* published in 1752 he described the capture of an unusual animal:

There is a report, but not altogether to be depended upon, that some peasants at Sundmoer have catched a Snake lately in a net, which was three fathoms long, and had four legs: this must somewhat resemble a crocodile. The peasants ran away frightened, and left the Snake to do the same.

As the Bishop points out, the value of this report is doubtful, but the animal described sounds very similar to the type of sea serpent reported in Norwegian waters (see figure 14, page 70). Its relatively small size — 18 feet [5.5 metres] — suggests that it might have been a young specimen.

After this brief report there seems to be little of interest until the autumn of 1808, when the carcase of a huge animal was washed up at Rothiesholm Point on the Isle of Stronsay in the Orkneys. The first man to notice it seems to have been a farmer from Dounatoun called John Peace, who was out fishing when the clamour of wheeling sea birds drew his attention to what he first thought was a dead whale. Most of the carcase was still in the water but several days later a storm threw the remains up on the beach. Word soon went round about the monster, which was said to have a small head, long neck and tail, and some sort of mane. Peace went back to examine the remains, which were rapidly decomposing, with George Sherar and Thomas Fotheringhame, a local carpenter. Each measured the beast and all agreed that its length was 55 feet [16.5 metres]. The most detailed description came from George Sherar who said on oath:

That the length of the neck was exactly fifteen feet, from the same hole to the beginning of the mane: That he measured also the circumference of the animal as accurately as he could, which was about ten feet, more or less; and the whole body, where the limbs were attached to it, was about the same circumference: That the lower jaw or mouth was awanting; but there were some substances or bones of the jaw remaining, when he first examined it, which are now away: That it had two holes on each side of the neck, beside the one on the back of the skull: That the mane or bristles were about fourteen inches in length each, of a silvery colour, and particularly luminous in the dark, before they were dried: That the upper part of the limbs, which answers to the shoulder-blade, was joined to the body like the shoulder-blade of a cow, forming part of the side: That a part of the tail was awanting, being incidentally broken off at the extremity; where the last joint of it was bare, was an inch and a half in breadth: That the bones were of a gristly nature like those of a halibut, the back-bone excepted, which was the only solid one in the body: That the tail was quite flexible, turning in every direction, as he lifted it; and he supposes the neck to have been equally so from its appearance at the time:

That there were either five or six toes on each paw, about nine inches long, and of a soft substance: That the toes were separated from each other and not webbed, so far as he was able to observe; and that the paw was about half a foot each way in length and breadth.

Fotheringhame added that 'The skin seemed to be elastic when compressed, and of a greyish colour, without any scales; it was rough to the feeling, on drawing the hand over towards the head, but was smooth as velvet when the hand was drawn towards the tail.' The creature's innards hung out from its body and the stomach discharged a reddish, fetid substance when opened. To cut a long story short, a drawing was made, depicting the carcase with six legs, and sent with affidavits from the witnesses and pieces of the bones and vertebrae to Everard Home, a London surgeon and keen naturalist. Strangely enough, Home had recently been engaged in studying the basking shark, a specimen of which had become entangled in fishermen's nets at Hastings. On reading the reports, Home was struck with several details which were consistent with those of a *Squalus,* and on examining the remains his suspicions were confirmed. What had been shown on the drawing as legs were two pairs of fins and the claspers, or male reproductive organs. These claspers are a feature of the sharks, skates, rays and chimaeras, a class known as the *Selachians.* The 'mane' was merely fibres of the flesh and muscle. The diet of the basking shark being plankton results in the stomach being full of a red fluid, which was that found in the stomach of the Stronsay beast. The creature's anatomy tallied in every way with a basking shark except one – the huge size. The largest known *Squalus* is 40 feet [12 metres] and such lengths seem rare. The Stronsay beast was measured separately by three men and found to be 55 feet [16.5 metres] long. Another species of shark, the whale shark, can reach such lengths but inhabits only warm waters, thousands of miles from the Orkneys. Home took a rather high-handed attitude, dismissing the measurements and saying that the remains were those of a 30 foot [9 metres] specimen. In fact, the huge vertebrae, each about 6 inches [15 centimetres] across, some of which are in the possession of the Royal Scottish Museum of Edinburgh, confirm the reported length. Home went further and rashly identified the creature as a common *Squalus maximus,* though it is impossible to identify a shark exactly without the teeth and the spicules from the skin, and these were not available to Home. The Stronsay beast was almost certainly a selachian, but its exact identity will never be known.

Throughout the nineteenth century the arguments for and against the possibility of sea serpents waxed furiously in the pages of natural history journals. One of these was *Land and Water,* and in the January issue of 1878 appeared an article about sea serpents by Dr Andrew Wilson. He included an account of a sea monster that had been washed ashore on the south-west coast of China in 1861. Captain Boyle of the schooner *Beaver* went to look at the beast and entered this report in his log:

> I came to anchor about twelve o'clock last night, about two miles out of this harbour. At half past four o'clock this morning I went on shore with five young Chinese. The villages that are about three miles up the river were all in uproar. I could not make out what was the matter with them – in fact, I thought it was another fight. A little while longer, I saw them dragging at something, but what it was I could not tell . . . When I got a little closer I saw that it was a great fish of some kind. He was not dead then . . . There were about 3000 men and boys on the spot, everyone with a lance, spear, knife or chopper. More than half of these men were cutting and haggling at this monster. By the time I had been looking on, and walking round it, they managed to cut about forty feet off its tail or the small end of the monster, which is just the same as a snake's. I requested them to cut off its head, and said I would give them 500 cash to have a good look at the inside of its mouth. This was gladly accepted, while some were standing close to me as if they were out of wind with the hard work they had had with their choppers. I asked them how that fish came there. They told me that he came there at his own accord, and when on the sand made a fearful splashing and noise on the sand and water. At first

everyone of them were scared, until some of the fishermen ventured close to it, and called out that it was a very
large fish, and that it was theirs. This caused everyone to
run with whatever they could get to cut for himself. The
fish ran on the bank at three o'clock.

By this time the monster's head was cut off, but very
much disfigured. I had then to draw it up the bank out of
the water, and had the lower jaw cut off so as I could
examine the inside of the mouth. I found the inside of the
mouth to be just the same as a snake's, but it had three
rows of soft teeth all as even as anything could be, and
exactly the same size. They were movable, that is, I could
move them towards the lip and back. At the entrance to
the throat I found a strange sort of gridiron-shaped, tough
substance, up and down. It was covered with a sort of
reddish flesh which causes me to think that this monster
of the deep lives on suckson [he apparently means
plankton]. The snout was flat, the cheek or eyebrow stuck
out about two and a-half feet – at least two and a-half
times the length of my boot. The skin was one and a-half
inches thick only, but awful tough and of a dirty blue
colour. I should think there must have been many tons of
barnacles on this monster. Where the barnacles were taken
off there was a dirty white spot to be seen. As near as
possible, it was twenty seven yards long. The head is
exactly like a snake's but the eye was very like a hog's,
till it was perfectly dead. My boots not being waterproof,
and the sun being very hot, I was forced to leave, or I
should have remained there until it was all cut up and
weighed; but this I could not do.

This report seems to be genuine and the features mentioned
– the flat snout, triple rows of teeth, grille at the entrance to
the throat, plankton diet, and prominent eyes – suggest a
huge selachian, like that washed up at Stronsay in 1808.
However the general shape of the beast is more like that of an
eel, and it is possible that it was an unknown species of giant
eel that had become adapted to a plankton diet. The reported
length of the creature, 80 feet [24 metres], makes it considerably larger than the basking shark, or even the whale

shark, but quite apart from the size the animal was unlikely to have been one of these creatures, for basking sharks are unknown in warm waters and whale sharks have very distinctive features, such as a yellowish skin covered with black spots. We shall see later that, in addition to the sightings, there is material evidence to support the existence of a giant eel.

In 1880 the following article appeared in the *Sea Side Press,* an American journal:

S. W. Hanna, of Pemaquid, caught what might be called a young sea serpent in his nets the other day. It was about 25 feet long and 10 inches in diameter in the largest part, and was shaped like an eel. The head was flat, and the upper part projected out over the mouth, which was small and contained sharp teeth. It was dead when found.

In response to queries from several naturalists, Captain Hanna gave more details:

The skin was not like a scale-fish, but more like a dog-fish or shark, though a great deal finer in quality. I did not save the fish for the reason that I did not know what I had caught. In fact, I considered it a streak of ill-luck rather than good fortune, having torn my nets very badly and otherwise bothering me in my business.

The body was round or very near that form . . . the color of its back was of a slate or fish color; belly, greyish-white. . . . The head did resemble that of a shark, only more stunted, i.e., it did not lengthen out like the shark's. The mouth was very small, not any larger than the mouth of a good-sized dog-fish, with fine, briery teeth, located at the extreme end of the head or nose.

Captain Hanna also drew a sketch (see figure 20).

There is a rare and primitive species of shark – the frilled shark *Chlamydoselachus,* which is similar to Captain Hanna's fish, but only 6 feet [1.8 metres] long, and there are several differences which we can see by comparing the Captain's sketch with the following drawing of a *Chlamydoselachus.*

It could have been a shark of a similar but unknown larger species, or maybe even an unknown species of giant eel.

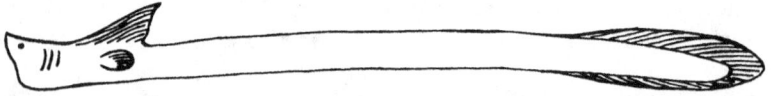

Figure 20 Captain Hanna's fish

Figure 21 Chlamydoselachus

In 1921 Dr A. Krempf, Director of the Oceanographic and Fisheries Service of Indo-China, reported the stranding of a giant carcase on the shore of Along Bay, Vietnam. The stranding, which occurred many years before in 1883, was described to him by Tran Van Con, a 56-year-old native of the region. The head was missing from the body which was about 60 feet [18 metres] long, 3 feet [1 metre] wide and covered with segmented armour, each segment having a pair of large fins. The body was dark brown above and yellowish below. The remains stank so much that the natives finally towed them out to sea. The description of this carcase is very similar to the reports by the French officers of the multi-finned creatures chased by their gunboats in the area (see figure 17, page 74).

In the spring of 1885 the Rev. Gordon of Milwaukee was visiting a remote part of the Atlantic shores of Florida. In the New River Inlet his anchor became fouled in a large rotting carcase. The length was about 42 feet [12.6 metres], its girth about 6 feet [1.8 metres]. The head was missing from the long, slender neck and there were two forelimbs or flippers. The intestines protruded from the decomposing body. To save the carcase from further destruction the Rev. Gordon dragged it up the beach, but soon after, unfortunately, a hurricane blew up and the elements reclaimed the creature. The beast might have been a big selachian, but there are no basking sharks in the warm waters of Florida. Whale sharks are known in this area but have a very distinctive colour and shape, and it is unlikely that their remains would resemble those found by the Rev. Gordon.

In the *Shipping Gazette* for 1886 there appeared an article about the capture of a sea serpent by a fishing boat, but there was no conclusion:

A sea serpent was reported to have been captured at Carabelle, Florida, by a fishing steamer named the *Crescent City* which it towed wildly for some time before it was killed. The thing measures 49 feet long and 6 feet in circumference. It is eel-shaped, with a shark-like head and a tail armed with formidable fins. It was caught with a shark-hook, but after being tired out it had to be shot.

On 1 November 1922 Hugh Balance of Natal, South Africa, told the press about a strange event he had witnessed some years previously.

I saw what I took to be two whales fighting with some sea monster about 1,300 yards from the shore. I got my glasses and was amazed to see what I took to be a polar bear, but of truly mammoth proportions. This creature I observed to rear out of the water fully twenty feet and to strike repeatedly with what I took to be its tail at the two whales, but with seemingly no effect.

This amazing story does not end here. After the battle, which lasted several hours and was watched by crowds from the shore, the whales swam off leaving the other creature dead on the surface. The next day the carcase was thrown up on the beach. It was about 47 feet [14 metres] long, 10 feet [3 metres] wide, and 5 feet [1.5 metres] high. It was covered in snow-white hair and had a trunk-like appendage about 5 feet [1.5 metres] long at one end. This creature lay

89

on the beach for several days, but was washed away by the spring tide before it could be examined by experts. It is hard to form any conclusion about this incident, but we have already seen how 'hair' can be formed on a carcase. The next report is more easily explained.

In 1925 the *World Wide* magazine published two photographs of a strange carcase washed ashore at Santa Cruz in California. The head was longer than a man, with a sort of beak, and was attached to the body by a long neck. The length was about 36 feet [11 metres]. The remains were badly decomposed. The skull was examined by the California Academy of Science, who pronounced it to be an extremely rare species of whale – *Berardius bairdi.*

There have been many eye witness reports of giant eel-like creatures and in 1930 came the capture of what seemed to be the larval form of one of these creatures, an eel larva which was 6 feet [1.8 metres] long! (See figure 22.) The larva was trawled up by the *Dana,* on an oceanographic expedition between the Cape and St Helena. The larva, or leptocephalus, of the common eel is 3 inches [7.5 centimetres] long maturing into an adult with a length of about 4 feet [1.2 metres]. The leptocephalus of the conger is 4 inches [10 centimetres] long giving rise to a 10 foot [3 metres] adult. Going by these proportions we would expect the giant leptocephalus to mature into an adult with a length of between 100 and 180 feet [30–54 metres]. However, recent research suggests that the giant leptocephalus belongs to the *Notocanthiformes,* deep sea fish which are not true eels, but closely related to them. The adult form is still unknown and might be of great size, but we cannot be certain. Once again, we are left with evidence that is not conclusive.

In February 1934 some fishermen found a huge rotting carcase on the beach at Querqueville, west of Cherbourg. It was about 20 feet [6 metres] long, with two front flippers, a small head and a long tapering tail. The body was covered with what looked like fur, and the beast's entrails were lying on the beach several yards away. It was examined thoroughly by Dr Georges Petit of the Paris Museum, who soon pronounced it to be a basking shark (see plate 14).

In December 1941 a decaying carcase was found at Deepdale

in the Orkneys. It was first described by Mr J. G. Marwick who went to view the remains with his brother. It had a small head, long neck, humped back and long tail. It also had two small projections on the skull, which looked like antennae. Mr Marwick, a keen naturalist, went back to retrieve some portions of the remains. He removed the skull and one of the forelimbs and preserved them in salt. He considered it to be the body of some sort of undiscovered marine saurian, and so sure was he that he gave it a name – *Scapasaurus* (Deepdale is in the vicinity of Scapa Flow).

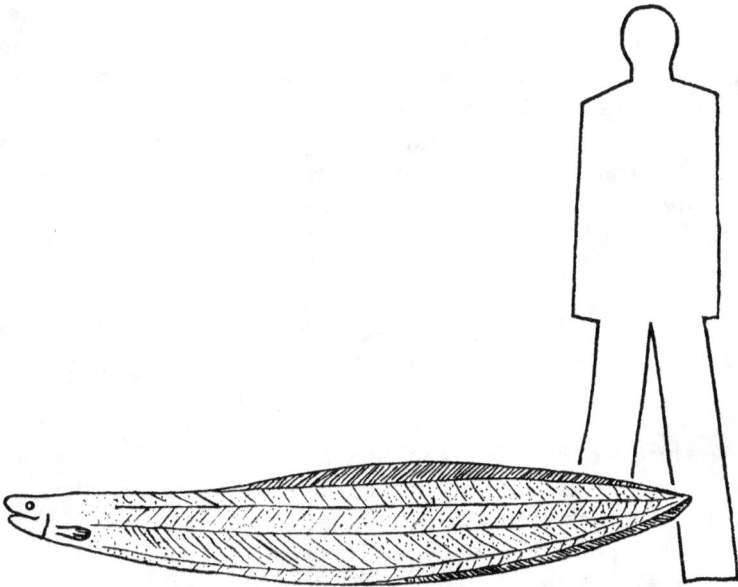

Figure 22 Giant leptocephalus (in comparison with 6-foot man)

A few weeks later a similar carcase was washed ashore at the Hope of Hunda, a few miles away. All that remained was a skull, backbone, and some cartilaginous fins. Like the Deepdale monster it had two antennae about 4 inches [10 centimetres] long.

Photographs of the two carcases were sent to the Natural History Museum, London, whose experts identified the creatures as basking sharks. The Royal Scottish Museum confirmed this view. This would have seemed to settle the matter, but, soon after this, Mr Marwick claimed that he had shown the remains to a biologist from Durham University, who was astounded and confirmed his opinion that the remains were those of an ancient type of sea reptile.

One wonders at the competence of the 'Durham biologist' for all the authorities identified the creatures as basking sharks. The local people were unconvinced by this explanation and one of the original viewers of the Deepdale monster wrote a letter to the *Orcadian,* one of the journals in which the case had been discussed. He wanted to know whether basking sharks had 'antennae' such as the Deepdale and Hunda specimens possessed. He received no answer but there is one. In the head of the basking shark the skull is extended forward into a narrow snout, which is supported by two rods – the rostral cartilages. It was these cartilages that formed the antennae on the Deepdale and Hunda monsters.

In 1947 the remains of a huge animal were washed ashore near Effingham, Vancouver Island. The carcase was about 40 feet [12 metres] long. As one might expect, it turned out to be the carcase of a basking shark, though, admittedly, a large one.

In 1957 the following article appeared in the *Daily Mail Yearbook*:

Mystery Monster: A giant hairy monster, with 6 foot tusks was washed ashore on the coast of Alaska in July 1956. The carcase, which was more than 100 feet long and 15 feet wide, had crimson flesh. Its origin and species were a complete mystery. Experts said that it fitted no known description of prehistoric beasts and that the 2 inch reddish brown hair which covered the thick decaying hide excluded any relationship to whales.

The monster was discovered by a veteran Alaskan hunting guide, and was apparently washed ashore during a gale in the Gulf of Alaska. Explorers who flew northward to view the carcase said that the Monster had a huge head measuring 5½ feet across, with eye sockets 9 inches wide and about 42 inches apart. Its teeth were 6 inches long and 5 inches wide at the base.

Clusters of ribs extended 6 feet from the spinal column, and the movable upper jaw, a solid tusk-like bone, protruded several feet beyond the end of the fixed lower jaw.

The carcase might have been that of a sperm whale, washed ashore upside down, whose tooth-filled lower jaw could have been taken for the upper jaw, but the reported length, considerably larger than the biggest sperm whales, seems to rule this out. Blue whales can attain such lengths but they have no teeth. The description might be exaggerated and inaccurate, and one wonders who the 'experts' were, for, as we have seen, 'hair' on such carcases is often caused by distintegrating fibres in the decaying flesh. We cannot be sure, but we would probably have heard more about this animal if it was as extraordinary as the account would have us believe.

Most of the carcases reported so far, however strange, at least bear some resemblance to living creatures, but this could not be said of the next case, a report of which appeared in the *Daily Telegraph* on 9 March 1962.

The body of a giant sea monster which has been washed up on the desolate West Tasmanian coast has baffled scientists. It is 20 feet long and 18 feet wide and has no defined head, eyes or other sense organs. It is believed the Monster was first seen on the beach two years ago but it was brought to the notice of scientists only a few days ago.

A party of scientists reported in Hobart that it had a frill and gill-like slits. They said the body was in an advanced stage of decomposition, but the flesh was extremely tough, like glass fibre and it had apparently been on the beach about twenty months. Its estimated live weight was about eight tons. The scientists believed the body was definitely not a mammal. Samples are being chemically analysed and more experts will probably be flown to the body soon.

This case had a very prosaic explanation, for an investigation soon revealed that this monster was merely an old, rotting mass of whale blubber, probably dumped by a whaling

93

ship. In 1965 a similar report appeared in Australia's *Townsville Bulletin*, describing a puzzling carcase that had been washed ashore at Auckland, New Zealand:

> Mystery Mass of Flesh and Hair – Auckland, N.Z. (A.A.P.)
> – Officials are puzzled over a huge, shapeless mass of flesh and hair which has appeared on the sand at Muriwai Beach here.
> The thing was first sighted a week ago by a Marine Department officer. Then the hairy blob of flesh was 30 feet long and 8 feet high. It is slowly being swallowed by the sand but more than 20 feet of it was still showing yesterday.
> Auckland University's zoology department head (Professor J. E. Morton) said: 'You can rule out whales because of the hair, and you can rule out sea elephants and sea cows because of its size.'
> The object has a tough quarter-inch thick hide. Under this is what appears to be a layer of fat, then solid meat. Hair four to six inches long covers its length.

Professor Morton was either mistaken or misquoted, for the zoology department of Auckland University soon revealed that the carcase was that of a whale, probably a Humpback whale.

Considering the many sightings of sea serpents, the amount of solid evidence is disappointing. Since the early eighteenth century there have been some 60 known captures or strandings of creatures which could be taken for sea serpents. Out of these there are only seven clear cases which probably refer to genuine unknown creatures. The most interesting of these are the creature netted at Sundmoer in the 1750s, which seems to have been a young specimen of one of the Scandinavian sea serpents, and the Along Bay Carcase of 1883, which was probably the remains of one of the Multi-finned sea serpents. Also there are the Stronsay carcase; Captain Boyle's carcase; Captain Hanna's fish; the *Crescent City*'s fish, and the giant leptocephalus, and these suggest that there are several species of giant eel, or giant eel-like selachian. Unfortunately, the only two cases of which we have specimens are the Stronsay carcase, and the giant leptocephalus and these alone are not conclusive proof of the existence of the sea serpents described in this book.

This disparity between the sightings and the lack of concrete evidence is one of the most puzzling aspects of the subject of sea serpents. What is the explanation? Part of the answer is probably that the anatomy of the sea serpents is sufficiently flexible and unspecialised to allow them to refloat themselves should they ever become stranded in shallow water, a fate which sometimes befalls the largest known sea creatures, the whales and giant squids, both of which are absolutely helpless out of water. Also it is unlikely that sea serpents would ever come so close to the shores. It seems that the main reason why whales are so frequently stranded is that their echo-sounding apparatus becomes ineffective if they stray into shallow waters, and their rigid bulk prevents them from taking stock of the situation by rearing out of the water, as sea serpents could do. So it seems that sea serpents are probably the least likely of sea creatures to be stranded, and, if they ever were, would be quite able to get off the shore without difficulty.

One rather outré theory put forward to explain the scarcity of concrete evidence is that the witnesses are describing exactly what they see, but that it is not part of the real world as we know it, rather, a manifestation of some other dimension which briefly overlaps our own. This is an interesting theory, but purely speculative, and, I feel, unnecessary. The sea is sufficiently vast to hold many mysteries, which, nevertheless, are part of the real world.

SEVEN
Other Curiosities

There are certain creatures and events which though not fitting directly into the narrative are still relevant to the subject. They suggest that the natural world still has many surprises for us.

Giant Squids

The story of the discovery of the giant squid presents an interesting parallel with that of the sea serpents and sheds much light on people's treatment of the unknown. Squids, cuttlefish and octopuses belong to the class *Cephalopoda,* and differ slightly in structure and habitat. The octopus has eight arms and a head closely joined to its sac-like body. It is built for crawling and normally inhabits crevices on the sea bed. The squid and cuttlefish have an extra pair of arms of great length which swell at the extremities into sucker-covered pads. Their bodies are long and streamlined, connected to the head by a short neck. Squids inhabit the open sea, chasing their prey at high speed, and, unlike octopuses, are helpless out of water, sometimes being stranded on beaches. The largest squids belong to the genus *Architeuthis,* which normally inhabits the North Atlantic. Today no one doubts the existence of the giant squid (see plate 15) but until the middle of the nineteenth century it was still widely regarded as a mythical beast, being confused with legends of the

97

Kraken, the Sea Orm, and floating islands. Those naturalists who did accept the possibility of such a creature were treated as cranks by the scientific establishment. One such man was Pierre Denys de Montfort, a brilliant but eccentric scientist. He collected many reports of the giant squid and studied as many fragments of its flesh and tentacles as he could obtain, finally writing about it at length in his book *Histoire naturelle des molluscs,* published in 1803. Alas, de Montfort's writings on the giant squid were regarded as the ravings of a madman and he was treated as such ever after. He became cynical and disillusioned, drifting from one menial job to another (no respectable establishment would employ him) and in the early 1820s he was found dead, apparently of drink, in a Paris gutter. He was 56 years old.

As the nineteenth century continued, evidence of the giant squid's existence accumulated, and one interested naturalist was the Dane, Johan Japetus Steenstrup. After assembling his evidence he read a paper on it to the society of Scandinavian Naturalists in 1847, and he seems to have convinced some members of the scientific world, but reports of squids more than 10 feet [3 metres] long were still widely treated with incredulity. What finally seemed to settle the issue was the stranding of many huge squids on the shores of Newfoundland in the 1870s. The biggest of these was that washed ashore at Thimble Tickle on 2 November 1878, its total length being about 60 feet [18 metres].

Figure 23 The Thimble Tickle squid

In most specimens the two long tentacles are relatively larger, being about three times the length of the body and head, as we can see from the specimen stranded at Labrador in 1873 (see figure 24).

The Thimble Tickle giant is the largest to be accepted by science but there are certainly larger ones. One was stranded on the coast of Iceland in 1555 with a reported length of 60 feet [18 metres] *without* the long tentacles which had become detached and lost. With them it would have been between 90 and 120 feet [27–36 metres] long. In 1924 the mutilated remains of another giant were washed ashore at Baven-on-Sea, Natal, South Africa, a report of which appeared in the *Natal Mercury*. All the tentacles were missing but the head and body were about 28 feet [8.4 metres] long, suggesting that the complete creature was between 80 and 110 feet [24–33 metres] in length. There is further evidence in the form of huge undigested portions of squid found in the stomachs of sperm whales. The largest of these pieces was that retrieved by Captain Reynolds in the early nineteenth century. This was a sucker-covered arm – not one of the two long tentacles – and was 45 feet [13.5 metres] long and 2ft 6 ins [75 centimetres] thick at the base. These arms usually occupy a quarter of the squid's total length so Reynolds's specimen could have come from a squid with a total length of about 180 feet [54 metres]. Later in the century Herman Melville describes such arms with a length of 30 feet [9 metres], and Frank Bullen, in his book *The Cruise of the 'Cachalot'* describes squids' arms as 'thick as a stout man's body' with suckers as large as saucers. In addition we have the sucker scars found on the skin of whales. The largest known scars are 18 inches [45 centimetres] in diameter, as described by Ivan T. Sanderson in his book *Follow the Whale*. The diameter of squids' suckers is usually one hundredth of the length of the body and head so we would expect 18-inch [45 centimetres] suckers to belong to a squid with a body and head 150 feet [45 metres] long and a total length, therefore, of between 500 and 600 feet [150–180 metres]! Of course these huge scars might well have come from squids with proportionally larger suckers but these beasts would still be immensely larger than those accepted by science.

Figure 24 The Labrador squid

From the foregoing we might expect that the octopus, though a somewhat different shape from the squid, would achieve giant size, but until recently there was no evidence for the existence of octopuses larger than *Paractopus apollyon*, which has a spread of about 30 feet [9 metres]. However a spectacular exception recently came to light. In the early 1960s F. G. Wood was researching the archives of the Laboratory of Marine Research in Florida, during which he found an account of the stranding of a huge cephalopod on the beach of St Augustine in 1897. The rotting remains had been examined by Professor Verrill, who estimated that the arms had been between 79 and 90 feet [24–27 metres] long! It was recorded that a piece of one of the tentacles had been preserved at the Smithsonian Institute. Wood located this specimen (after half a century!) in a barrel of formalin at the Institute and asked his friend Joseph F. Gennaro to analyse it. By examining the tissue under the microscope, comparing it with other cephalopod flesh, Gennaro established that the beast was a giant octopus, a creature some 100 feet [30 metres] long! So far as I know this case is unique.

Only a handful of people have been privileged to see one of these great beasts alive. They inhabit the deepest oceans and only occasionally are their rotting remains washed ashore. As we have seen, the giant squid was once regarded in the same light as sea serpents but its existence was eventually confirmed. We can only hope that the existence of sea serpents will soon be established so decisively.

The Capture of a 'Trold'

In 1752 *The Natural History of Norway,* by Bishop Erik Pontoppidan, was published. It is an accurate, objective work and much space is devoted to sea serpents, some of which are among those types described in this book. In one chapter is a puzzling footnote:

> Anno 1744 one Dagfind Korsbeck catched, in the parish of Sundelvems on Sundmoer, a monstrous Fish, which many people saw at his house. It's head was almost like

the head of a cat; it had four paws, and about the body was a hard shell like a lobster's; it purred like a cat, and when they put a stick to it, would snap at it. The peasants looked upon it as a Trold, or ominous fish, and were afraid to keep it; and, consequently, a few hours later, they threw it into the sea again. According to the description, this might be called a Sea-Armadilla, by which name an American Land-Animal is known, nearly of the same shape, excepting that it has a long tail.

One presumes from the account that the animal was fairly small but its identity is a mystery.

Giant Penguin Tracks

In February 1948 a series of huge, three-toed footprints were found on the beaches of Clearwater in Florida. Each print was some 18 inches [45 centimetres] long, bird-like and of a depth which indicated a creature with a weight of from 2 to 3 tons. Shortly after there were several reports of a huge black creature waddling through the swamps and beaches of the area. Four air pilots claimed to have seen the beast and one reported 'Maybe I'm crazy . . . but that damned thing looked like a giant penguin to me.' Ivan T. Sanderson, a qualified zoologist and keen investigator of such phenomena, flew to the scene with a camera crew from NBC and undertook a detailed enquiry. Naturally the idea of a hoax occurred to him and he set about reproducing the footprints with the aid of some engineering friends. They eventually concluded that to make such footprints artificially one would need a complex machine weighing some 2 –3 tons yet manoeuvrable enough to bring through the surrounding woods and swamps without leaving traces. It would be very hard to control as only the imprint-making feet could touch the ground. The existence of a giant penguin-like bird seemed to be the most likely explanation. More footprints appeared on the coast that year, always emanating from the water and returning to it, and the sightings continued till about the end of October, when they ceased. Similar footprints have appeared on shores

in other parts of the world, and they reappeared on the
Florida coast in 1966. Sanderson stressed that the footprints
were very similar to those of a penguin, but the largest
known penguins were 6 feet [2 metres] tall, fossil remains of
which were recently found in New Zealand. Presumably the
maker of 18-inch [45 centimetres] footprints would be considerably larger.

Does Steller's Sea-cow still exist?

Marine mammals are divided into three groups: the *Cetacea*,
or whales; the *Pinnipeda*, or seals, and the *Sirenia*, which
comprises the Manatees, the Dugongs, and Steller's Sea-cow.
The Sirenians are placid herbivorous creatures, whose ancestry
is uncertain, and Steller's Sea-cow, from the North Pacific,
was thought to have become extinct in the mid-eighteenth
century. This huge creature was from 25 to 30 feet [7.5 –
9 metres] long, slow and defenceless, and unfortunately
shared its habitat with a species of fur seal. The discovery
of the seals brought hordes of hunters who indiscriminately
slaughtered the Sea-cows along with the seals, and by the
1750s it was apparently extinct. However, it later seemed
that the Sea-cow was more widespread than previously
thought. It was believed to be restricted to the Komandorskie
Islands, but in the 1830s there were more reports from
Bering Island following its colonisation, but eventually these
too ceased. Nothing more was heard until 1910 when there
was a rather vague report of a creature resembling a Sea-cow
being washed ashore at Cape Chaplin, in the Gulf of Anadyr,
but this was never confirmed. Again, there was nothing more
for many years, then in the early 1950s Dr S. K. Klumov, of
the Moscow Institute of Oceanology, heard a strange report
from the crew of one of the whaling boats from the Kurile
Islands. He described it in the journal *Priroda,* published by
the USSR Academy of Sciences:

In 1951 –56 I was working in the north-western Pacific,
engaged in the study of the whales of the Far East. I
visited the coastal whaling-stations in the Kurile Islands,

went to sea aboard the whalers, took part in the hunts and
met many of the whaling men, who are folk of great
experience. And one day, as I was standing on board with
some of them and we were watching a fairly big shark
swim past the ship, showing its great fin, the harpooner
Ivan Skripkin said to me: 'You're a scientist, eh? Will you
explain to me please what kind of beast it is that we have
seen almost every year for several years running not far
from the Komandorskie Islands? The creature always
appears at the very same place, and we always see it at the
same time: usually in the first half of July. The area is
not far from Komandor, say 30 miles [48 kilometres] or
so south-east of there, in the Pacific. We run into it once
or twice a year when we are whaling there. Of course it's
no whale. We know whales: you can tell a whale by its
appearance, its colour, its dorsal fin, and by the way it
blows.

This thing doesn't blow, and it doesn't stick its head
out of the water, but, like that shark there, it only shows
the top part of its back. The back is enormous, very wide,
and smooth, with no fins at all, and black in colour. . . .
It's a good 10 metres (30 feet) long, if I'm not mistaken,
and I don't think my eye deceives me.

In 1962 there was a similar report from the whaler *Buran*,
of some strange creatures seen by the crew near Cape Navarin,
in July of that year. The ship was near the coast one morning
when a group of unusual animals was seen about 100 yards
[90 metres] away. They were seen again the following day,
and were about 25 feet [7.5 metres] long, dark in colour,
and with horizontal tails edged with a fringe. They swam
slowly along in a compact group, occasionally diving. This
encounter was described by three Russian naturalists
A. A. Berzin, E. A. Tikhomirov and V. I. Troinin, in *Priroda*.
Both Klumov's report and the *Buran*'s report suggest that the
Sea-cow still exists. The three naturalists wrote:

As we know, the sea-cow was completely exterminated in
the Komandorskie Islands by fur-seal hunters. However, in
other areas, where the sea-cow may have lived, if we are to

judge from the data we have cited, there was no hunting of this kind, because there were no animals with valuable fur. We may suppose that the sea-cow could have survived there . . .

Figure 25 Steller's Sea-cow

The Capture of a Mermaid

On 21 July 1961 the *Shetland Times* printed an article under the heading 'Did the Mermaid Exist?' It was concerned with the reported capture of a mermaid by fishermen in 1833. The account was written by Arthur Nicholson, JP, of Lochend, and found in an assortment of old documents by Lady Nicholson.

In the presence of Arthur Nicholson of Lochend, J.P. – William Manson, Daniel Manson, John Henderson, residing in Cullivoe in the parish of North Yell, who being sworn deposit – That, in the beginning of the month of July last, they at the deep-sea fishing from 30 to 60 miles from land, and about midnight took up a creature attached by the back of the neck to a hook, which was about 3 feet long, and about 30 inches in circumference at the broadest part, which was across the shoulders. From the navel upwards it resembled a human being – had breasts as large as those of a woman. Attached to the side were arms about 9 inches long, with wrists and hands like those of a human being, except that there were webs between the fingers for about

104

half their length. The fingers were in number and shape, like those of a man. The little arms were close on the outsides of the breasts and on the corner of each shoulder was placed a fin of a round form which, when extended, covered both the breasts and the arms. The animal had a short neck, on which rested a head, about the length of a man's but not nearly so round; and somewhat pointed at the top. It had eyebrows without hair, and eyelids covering two small blue eyes, somewhat like those of a human being – not like those of a fish. It had no nose, but two orifices for blowing through. It had a mouth so large that when opened wide it would admit a man's fist. It had lips rather thicker than a man's of a pure white colour. There was no chin, but they think the lower jaw projected a little further than the upper one. There were no ears. The whole front of the animal was covered with skin, white as linen, the back with skin of a light-grey colour, like a fish. From the breasts the shape sloped towards the tail, close to which was only about 4 inches in circumference. The tail was flat, and consisted of two lobes which, when extended, might be 6 inches together in breadth, and were set at right angles with the face of the creature; It resembled the tail of a halibut. The animal was very nearly round at the shoulders. It appeared to have shoulder bones and a hollow space between them. The diminution of size increased most rapidly from the navel, which might be 9 inches below the breasts. There was between the nostrils a thing that appeared to be a piece of gristle about 9 inches long, and which resembled a thick bristle. There was a similar one on each side of the head, but not so long, which the animal had the power of moving backwards and forwards, and could make them meet on top of the skull. When the men spoke the animal answered, and moved these bristles, which led them to suppose that the creature heard by means of them. They did not observe what sort of teeth the creature had, nor the parts of generation. There was no hair upon any part of its body which was soft and slimy.

There is an old opinion among fishermen that it is unlucky to kill a mermaid and therefore, after having kept it in the boat for some time, they slipped it.

All of which is the truth, so help me God.

The skipper of the boat also described the incident to one Mr Edmondston, who sent an account to the Natural History Department at Edinburgh University. He said:

Not one of the six men dreamed of a doubt of its being a mermaid. . . . The usual resources of scepticism that the seals and other sea animals appearing under certain circumstances operating upon an excited imagination and so producing an ocular illusion cannot avail here. It is quite impossible that six Shetland fishermen could commit such a mistake.

Now the accepted explanation of mermaids is that they are really members of that strange marine family the Sirenians, which comprise the manatees, dugongs and Steller's Sea-cow (the latter now believed extinct). The dugong seems to be the most likely, having a bilobate tail, a relatively hairless body and two front flippers. It has been seen to suckle its young while standing half out of the water and one can see how this could give rise to stories of mermaids. However, none of the Sirenians is indigenous to Scottish waters and it seems impossible to reconcile the hideously ugly dugong with the fishermen's detailed description of their mermaid. It does not give the impression of a hoax. Tim Dinsdale has tentatively put forward the suggestion that the experience may have been some sort of collective hallucination. This seems more likely than the existence of a creature which is half-maiden and half-fish – an animal too improbable even for me!

A Note on 'Nessie'

So far only marine beasts have been discussed, but for many years there have been reports of freshwater monsters from all over the world. The subject of freshwater monsters really deserves a book to itself but brief mention should be made of one famous phenomenon, the Loch Ness Monster.

Since the time of St Columba, about AD 560 there have

been reports of a monster with a long neck and bulky body in Loch Ness, which would seem to offer a particularly suitable home for such creatures. It is about 28 miles [44.8 kilometres] long, 700 feet [210 metres] deep in parts, and contains some 263,000 million cubic feet of water. This enormous volume of water collects enough heat during the summer to keep the deeper parts at about 5.5°C all year round so there are no uncomfortable extremes of temperature. Assuming the creatures to be carnivorous they would have a more than adequate diet, the Loch containing large stocks of trout, salmon, char, and enormous shoals of eels.

How long have the monsters been in Loch Ness? It seems certain that they arrived a long time ago and are confined there. The only access routes to the sea, the Caledonian Canal and the River Ness, are too small and busy to allow the passage of large creatures. Also, any creatures coming up the River Ness would encounter the obstacle of Telford's Weir. It has been suggested that the Loch might be connected to the sea by underwater channels, the monsters entering periodically, but this is very improbable. The surface of Loch Ness is 52 feet [15.6 metres] above sea level so if the underwater tunnels were of any size the water in the Loch would have sunk to the level of the sea. If the tunnels were small, unable to balance the inflow to the Loch from burns and rivers, the current through them would be too strong to allow their blind negotiation for several miles by any large sea creatures. A solution to the problem is suggested by the geological structure of the area. This part of Scotland is rising very slowly, a process which began 10,000 years ago when the huge covering of ice from the Ice Age started to melt. The process continued so that the Great Glen, once submerged, rose clear forming Loch Ness which was still an arm of the sea. During this period the Loch might have offered advantages to sea dwellers, such as an abundance of prey and a refuge from ocean-going predators. Creatures, including the monsters, who visited the Loch might have been disinclined to leave it and stayed there while the land rose still further severing the link with the sea.

The evidence in the case of the Loch Ness Monster differs in one important way from that of the sea serpents, for much of it is the result of deliberate research, rather than just random sightings. There is continual surveillance of the Loch by dedicated bands of enthusiasts, and there have been several organised expeditions to the Loch. Probably the most important are those undertaken since 1967, when, due to the interest and perseverance of Professor Roy Mackal of Chicago University, the Field Enterprises Educational Corporation of Chicago donated a research grant of 20,000 dollars to the Loch Ness Investigation. This was really a turning point in the Loch Ness story for it brought the beginnings of scientific respectability to the case, encouraging reticent scientists to voice their opinions openly without fear of ridicule. The results of these recent investigations were summarised in Professor Mackal's book *The Monsters of Loch Ness,* published in 1976.

Mackal examines very critically the films and photographs of the Loch Ness Monster, and, while dismissing some, accepts others as a true record of large unknown creatures. Probably the most important of these is the film obtained by Tim Dinsdale in 1960, which shows what seems to be the monster moving across the Loch. This film was analysed in 1965 by the British Joint Air Reconaissance Intelligence Centre – JARIC – regarded as one of the world's most expert interpreters of photography. Their conclusion was that the film was genuine and showed a large animate object, certainly not a boat, moving across the surface of Loch Ness at about 11 mph [17.6 kph].

Mackal's team also obtained recordings of some very strange noises deep in the Loch. Letting down hydrophones they heard repeated clicking noises, which did not have a regular cycle and which sometimes seemed to come from several sources. These clicking sounds were often accompanied by swishing noises, such as would be produced by big animals swimming through the water. Several marine animals use sonar techniques in dark waters to communicate, navigate and hunt food. (The waters of Loch Ness are opaque below a few yards due to a heavy concentration of peat.) The noises from Loch Ness are quite different from any produced by known creatures.

Another important aspect of the Loch Ness case is the

evidence obtained from sonar trackings, both from shore-based equipment and boats. This is reproduceable evidence and shows that there are several large objects moving in the depths of Loch Ness. These appear, not just individually, but in small groups and they seem to be in the region of 20 feet [6 metres] long. Speeds of up to 17 mph [27.3 kph] have been recorded.

The eye witness accounts give us a clear picture of the beast's appearance. The head is proportionately very small and connected by a long neck to a bulky body. Several sightings mention flippers – both fore and aft – sometimes actually seen above water and sometimes inferred from the wash surrounding the shoulders and rump of the animal. Some reports, including the terrestrial sightings near the edge of the Loch, describe a large, blunt tail. The colour is usually given as grey or brown, the skin seeming rough in texture. A small number of reports mention fur, though as pointed out in chapter 5 'hair' might be filaments of flesh, as in the hairy frog. Occasionally reports talk of a pair of small horns on the head.

The question of the Monster's identity is a knotty one. Most experts rule out the possibility of it being an invertebrate or a fish. It could be an amphibian, a reptile like a plesiosaur, or a mammal, possibly being related to the long-necked type of sea serpent, which seems to be a pinniped. The arguments will rage on, but I think it is more important that serious investigation is taking place, increasingly with the support of the scientific world. If the existence of the Loch Ness Monster, confined in a lake in a densely populated country, is proved it will make the existence of such creatures in the vast sea seem much more likely.

Chronological Table
of Sightings

Chronological Table of Sightings

Date		Location	Witnesses	Probable type
1660s	?	Norwegian coast	Burgomaster of Malmö	Scandinavian Giant Otter
1687		Dramsfjord, Norway	Several people	Scandinavian Giant Otter
1734	6 July	Godthaab, Greenland	Hans Egede	Scandinavian Giant Otter
1740s	?	Sarica, Sicily	Fishermen	Giant Eel
1744		Sundmör, Norway	Dagfind Korsbeck	Scandinavian Giant Otter
1746	August	Jule Naess, Norway	Von Ferry and others	Scandinavian Giant Otter
1750s	?	Sundsland, Norway	Fishermen	Scandinavian Giant Otter
1750s	?	Heröy, Norway	Mr Tuchsen	Scandinavian Giant Otter
1750s	?	Sundmör, Norway	Peasants	Scandinavian Giant Otter
1759	?	Bergen, Norway	Norwegian Captain	Scandinavian Giant Otter
1763	?	Bergen, Norway	Norwegian Captain	Scandinavian Giant Otter
1779		Penobscot Bay, Maine, USA	Captain Williams and crew of the *Protector*	Long-necked Seal
1779		Penobscot Bay, Maine, USA	Stephen Tuckey	Undefined Extension
1781		Near or in Baltic	Sir Alexander Ball	Scandinavian Giant Otter
1786	1 August	North-east of the Azores	Crew of the *General Coole*	Undefined Extension
1793	20 June	Penobscot Bay, Maine, USA	E. Crabtree	Undefined Extension
1799		Penobscot Bay, Maine, USA	Two young men	Long-necked Seal
1800s	?	Cape Breton, Newfoundland, Canada	W. Lee	Multi-humped
1802	July	Cape Rosoi, Long Island	Rev. Abraham Cummings	Waterhorse
1808	June	Coll, Outer Hebrides	Rev. Donald Maclean	Waterhorse
1808	June	Canna, Outer Hebrides	13 boats	Waterhorse

Year	Date	Location	Observer	Type
1808	?	East coast of USA	Captain Lillis	Undefined Extension
1815	20 June	Cape Cod, Mass., USA	Captain E. Finney and others	Multi-humped
1815	21 June	Cape Cod, Mass., USA	Captain E. Finney	Multi-humped
1817	6 August	Gloucester, Mass., USA	Two women and some fishermen	Multi-humped
1817	10 August	Gloucester, Mass., USA	Amos Story	Multi-humped
1817	12 August	Gloucester, Mass., USA	Solomon Allen III	Multi-humped
1817	13 August	Gloucester, Mass., USA	Solomon Allen III	Multi-humped
1817	14 August	Gloucester, Mass., USA	Mathew Gafney and others	Multi-humped
1817	15 August	Gloucester, Mass., USA	James Mansfield	Multi-humped
1817	16 August	Cape Ann, Mass., USA	Colonel Perkins and Mr Lee and crew of nearby ship	Multi-humped
1817	17 August	Gloucester, Mass., USA	William Foster and 4 men in nearby boat	Multi-humped
1817	18 August	Gloucester, Mass., USA	William Pearson and friend	Multi-humped
1817	23 August	Gloucester, Mass., USA	Amos Story	Multi-humped
1817	28 August	Cape Ann, Mass., USA	Captain Toppan and crew of the *Laura*	Multi-humped
1817	3 October	Long Island Sound, USA	J. Guion	Multi-humped
1817	5 October	Long Island Sound, USA	T. Hertell	Multi-humped
1818	?	Mageroy Sound, Finmark, Norway	A gravedigger	Scandinavian Giant Otter
1818	?	North Cape, Finmark, Norway	Fishermen	Scandinavian Giant Otter
1818	?	Trondhjem, Tröndelag, Norway	Bishop of Nordland and Finmark	Scandinavian Giant Otter
1818	?	Foldenfjord, Tröndelag, Norway	Fishermen	Scandinavian Giant Otter
1818	?	Between Faroes and Hebrides	Captain Brown	Long-necked Seal

113

Date	Location	Witnesses	Probable type
1818 27 June	Portland, Maine, USA	Fishermen	Giant Eel
1818 11 July	Portland, Maine, USA	Several gentlemen	Giant Eel
1818 23 July	Gloucester, Mass., USA	Fishermen	Multi-humped
1818 25 July	Gloucester, Mass., USA	W. Sargent	Multi-humped
1818 30 July	Gloucester, Mass., USA	Captain Webber and others	Multi-humped
1818 12 August	Gloucester, Mass., USA	T. Hodgkins and 3 friends	Multi-humped
1818 16 August	Squam, Mass., USA	Many people	Multi-humped
1818 19 August	Squam, Mass., USA	Captain Rich and others	Multi-humped
1819 6 June	Race Point, Mass., USA	Crew of the *Concord*	Multi-humped
1819 July	Hordaland, Norway	Captain Schilderup and others	Scandinavian Giant Otter
1819 August	Nordland, Norway	John Gregor and others	Scandinavian Giant Otter
1819 13 August	Nahant, Mass., USA	James Prince and a crowd of 200 people	Multi-humped
1819 August	Nahant, Mass., USA	Nathan Chase and others	Multi-humped
1819 26 August	Gloucester, Mass., USA	Crew of the *Science*	Multi-humped
1819	Massachusetts Bay, USA	Several People	Multi-humped
1820	Hundholm, Tröndelag, Norway	Fishing boat skipper	Scandinavian Giant Otter
1820 5 August	Swampscott, Mass., USA	Andrew Reynolds and 3 friends	Multi-humped
1820 ?	North Atlantic	Crew of the *Lady Combermere*	Long-necked Seal
1821 2 August	Portsmouth, New Hampshire, USA	Samuel Duncan and others	Multi-humped
1822 ?	Scottish coast	Friend of Sir Walter Scott	Waterhorse

Year	Date	Location	Observer(s)	Category
1822		Soröy Island, Finmark, Norway	Many people	Scandinavian Giant Otter
1823	July	Gurnet, Mass., USA	The Weston brothers	Multi-humped
1823	12 July	Nahant, Mass., USA	Francis Johnson, Jr	Multi-humped
1824		Several miles off Uruguay	Friend of Professor Silliman	Waterhorse
1824	11 August	Portsmouth, Mass., USA	The Ruggles Family	Multi-humped
1825	15 July	Halifax, Nova Scotia, Canada	Mr Goreham and others	Multi-humped
1826	16 June	Newfoundland, Canada	Mr Warbourton on the *Silas Richards*	Multi-humped
1827	August	Oslofjord, Norway	Several people	Scandinavian Giant Otter
1828	?	South Atlantic	Captain F. W. Beechey of the *Blossom*	Undefined Extension
1829		off Cape of Good Hope	Captain Petrie of the *Royal Saxon*	Undefined Extension
1829		Oslofjord, Norway	Lars Johnoen	Waterhorse
1830	23 March	Charleston, S. Carolina	Crew of the *Eagle*	Sea Saurian
1830		Kennebec, Maine, USA	Mr Gooch and others	Multi-humped
1831		Long Island, New York	Several gentlemen	Multi-humped
1832		Nordland, Norway	Many people	Long-necked Seal
1833		Mahone Bay, Nova Scotia, Canada	Captain Sullivan and others	Multi-humped
1834		Castine, Maine, USA	Crew of a schooner	Long-necked Seal
1835		Gloucester, Mass., USA	Captain Shibbles and the crew of the *Mangehan*	Waterhorse
1837		Tröndelag, Norway	?	Waterhorse
1840s	?	Gulf of California	Captain George Hope and crew of HMS *Fly*	Sea Saurian

115

Chronological Table of Sightings

Date	Location	Witnesses	Probable type
1840s	Kristiansund, Norway	Nils Ree	Waterhorse
1840s	Kristiansund, Norway	John Johnson	Scandinavian Giant Otter
1840s	Kristiansund, Norway	Wilhelm Knudtzen and others	Waterhorse
1840s	Kristiansund, Norway	Mr Gaeschke	Waterhorse
1840s	Between Iceland and the Faroes	Captain Christmas	Long-necked Seal
1840s	Romsdalfjord, Norway	A priest	Scandinavian Giant Otter
1840	Gulf of Mexico	Captain Dabnour and crew of *Ville de Rochfort*	Multi-humped
1844	Arisaig, Nova Scotia, Canada	Mr Barry	Multi-humped
1845	Romsdalfjord, Norway	Mr Lund and others	Scandinavian Giant Otter
1845	Merigomish, Nova Scotia, Canada	Two people	Multi-humped
1845	Bergen, Norway	J. D. M. Sterling and others	Scandinavian Giant Otter
1846	Virginia, USA	Captain Lawson	Multi-finned
1846	Cape Cod, Mass., USA	B. H. Revoil and others	Multi-humped
1846	St Margaret, Nova Scotia, Canada	James Wilson and James Boehner	Waterhorse
1846	Bjornfjord, Norway	Daniel Salomonson and others	Scandinavian Giant Otter
1848	Between St Helena and the Cape	Captain M'Quae and the crew of HMS *Daedalus*	Long-necked Seal
1848	West of Oporto, Portugal	Officer and crew of HMS *Plumper*	Long-necked Seal

Year	Date	Location	Witnesses	Classification
1849	18 February	Florida, USA	Captain Adams and crew of the *Lucy and Nancy*	Undefined Extension
1849		St Margaret, Nova Scotia, Canada	Joseph Holland and others	Unclassifiable
1850s	?	Greiss Bay, Sutherland, Scotland	Mrs M'Iver	Long-necked Seal
1850s	?	Plymouth, Mass., USA	A gentleman	Multi-humped
1850s	?	Scottish coast	Andrew Strang	Long-necked Seal
1850s	?	Gulf of Bengal	Crew and passengers of the *Nemesis*	Sea Saurian
1850		Between Barcelona and Havana	Crew of Catalan frigate	Long-necked Seal
1852		Off West African coast	Captain W. Taylor and crew of the *Peggy*	Undefined Extension
1852	28 August	Off South African coast	Crew and passengers of the *Barham*	Multi-finned
1854	8 March	Singapore	Crew and passengers of the *Benjamin*	Unclassifiable
1854		Savannah, Georgia	Crews of the *William Seabrook* and the *Isabel*	Long-necked Seal
1854		St Helena	Grandfather of Captain de Weerdt	Waterhorse
1856	30 March	North Atlantic	Captain Guy, crew and passengers of the *Imogen*	Multi-humped
1856	8 July	South Africa	Captain Tremearne and crew of the *Princess*	Multi-finned
1857	16 February	Cape Town	Dr Biccard and others	Unclassifiable
1857	12 December	St Helena	Captain G. H. Harrington and crew of the *Castilian*	Giant Eel

Date		Location	Witnesses	Probable type
1858	26 January	Between St Helena and Cape Town	Captain Suckling of the *Carnatic*	Undefined Extension
1861		Ushant, Brittany	Captain Anderson and crew of the *Delta*	Long-necked Seal
1863	6 May	Between Canaries and Cape Verde Islands	Crew and passengers of the *Athenian*	Waterhorse
1864	?	St Margaret, Nova Scotia	W. Crooks and his son	Long-necked Seal
1870	15 October	Norfolk Island	John Adams and others	Giant Eel
1871		Kilkee, Co. Clare, Ireland	Several people	Waterhorse
1872	13 May	Gulf of Mexico	Captain A. Hassel and crew of the *St Olaf*	Multi-finned
1872	26 July	Cape Coast, Ghana	Captain H. M. Dyer of HMS *Torch*	Giant Eel
1872	20 August	Between Skye and Scotland	Rev. Macrae, his daughters, grandson, and Rev. Twopenny	Multi-humped
1872	21 August	Between Skye and Scotland	Rev. Macrae, his daughters, grandson, and Rev. Twopenny	Multi-humped
1872	23 August	Loch Duich	Alexander Macmillan and others	Multi-humped
1872	24 August	Loch Duich	Alexander Macmillan and others	Multi-humped
1873	20 March	West Indies	Captain Perry and crew of the *Orontes*	Undefined Extension
1873	17 September	Golspie, Sutherland, Scotland	Dr Soutar	Long-necked Seal

Year	Date	Location	Observer(s)	Classification
1873	18 September	Golspie, Sutherland, Scotland	Rev. James Joass	Long-necked Seal
1873	18 November	Firth of Forth, Scotland	120 people	Giant Eel
1875	8 July	Cape San Roque, Brazil	Captain Drevar and crew of the *Pauline*	Giant Eel
1875	13 July	Cape San Roque, Brazil	Captain Drevar and crew of the *Pauline*	Giant Eel
1875	17 July	Plymouth, Mass., USA	Captain Garton of the *Norman*	Multi-humped
1875	30 July	Swampscott, Mass., USA	Several people on yacht *Princess*	Multi-humped
1876	11 September	Malacca Straits	Captain Webster, crew and passengers of the *Nestor*	Giant Tadpole
1877	21 May	West of Sumatra	Crew of the *Georgina*	Giant Tadpole
1877	2 June	Cape Vito, Sicily	Captain L. Pearson and officers of Royal Yacht *Osborne*	Multi-finned
1877	15 July	Gloucester, Mass., USA	George S. Wasson and B. L. Fernald on Wasson's yacht *Gulnare*	Multi-humped
1877	30 July	North Atlantic	Captain W. H. Nelson and the helmsman of the *Sacramento*	Sea Saurian
1878		Aden or Suez	Mrs Turner on the *Poonah*	Multi-finned
1878		New Caledonia, Barrier Reef	Crew of the *Seudre*	Waterhorse
1879	28 January	Gulf of Aden	Some passengers and crew of the *City of Baltimore*	Undefined Extension
1879	30 March	Géographe Bay, Western Australia	Rev. H. W. Brown and Mr and Mrs M'Guire	Multi-finned
1879	5 August	100 miles west of Brest, France	Captain J. F. Fox of the *Privateer*	Giant Eel

119

Date		Location	Witnesses	Probable type
1879	21 December	Cape San Lewis, California, USA	G. Verschuur on the *Grenada*	Undefined Extension
1879		Indian Ocean	Dr C. H. Caldicott of the *Priam*	Undefined Extension
1880	11 August	North Pacific	Captain Thomas U. Brocklehurst of the *Oceanic*	Giant Tadpole
1880	?	Ningpo, China	J. H. Hoar	Giant Eel
1880	?	Suva, Fiji	Major James Harding	Waterhorse
1880	?	Near Melbourne	Captain A. Cooper and crew of the *Carlisle Castle*	Waterhorse
1881	12 November	Cape Town, South Africa	C. M. Hansen, his family and several neighbours	Waterhorse
1882	31 May	Near the Hebrides	Captain Weisz and crew of the *Käte*	Multi-humped
1882	3 September	Ormes Head, Wales	W. Barfoot and others	Long-necked Seal
1883	26 July	Libreville, Gabon	Captain Hollman and crew of *Elisabeth*	Long-necked Seal
1883		Las Perlas Archipelago, Panama	Captain Seymour and crew of *Hope On*	Long-necked Seal
1883		Bristol Channel	?	Long-necked Seal
1883		Newfoundland Banks	Crew of American schooner	Giant Turtle
1884	31 August	Durban, Natal, South Africa	Captain Wellington and crew of the *Churchill*	Undefined Extension
1885	5 August	North Atlantic	Captain Roberts of the *Emblem*	Undefined Extension
1885	16 August	Nordland, Norway	Some lads	Scandinavian Giant Otter
1885	4 October	Umhlali, Natal, South Africa	Several people	Giant Tadpole

Year	Date	Location	Witness	Classification
1886	29 August	Hudson River, New Jersey, USA	Two people	Giant Eel
1886	August	East coast of USA	Mr Jonah	Undefined Extension
1886		Red Sea	Officer and paymaster of *Le Parseval*	Undefined Extension
1887	30 July	Shuna, Argyll, Scotland	Professor M. F. Heddle and Mr J. H. Brown	Unclassifiable
1888	30 September	Red Sea	Crew of the *Messir*	Undefined Extension
1889	1 September	Madagascar	Crew of the *Meurthe*	Unclassifiable
1889		Between Gibraltar and Algiers	Anonymous Captain	Long-necked Seal
1890		Long Island, Conn., USA	Captain David Tuits of the *Anny Harper*	Undefined Extension
1891	14 July	North Island, New Zealand	A. F. Matthews on the *Manapouri*	Undefined Extension
1891		North Island, New Zealand	Captain A. L. Kerr and the quartermaster of the *Rotomahana*	Undefined Extension
1892	3 October	Firth of Tay, Angus	Crew of the *Catherine*	Undefined Extension
1892		Near Lagos, Nigeria	Crew of the *Angola*	Waterhorse
1892		West coast of France	Edward Rockliff and others	Undefined Extension
1893		Along Bay, Vietnam	Crew of *La Mutine*	Multi-finned
1893		Lochalsch, Scotland	Dr Farquehar Matheson and his wife	Long-necked Seal
1893	4 December	Cape Blanc, Mauretania	Captain Cringle and mate of the *Umfuli*	Long-necked Seal
1894	July	Hammerfest, Finmark, Norway	Several crews	Scandinavian Giant Otter
1895	7 February	Lewis, Hebrides	Angus Macdonald	Multi-humped

Date	Location	Witnesses	Probable type
1895	Lewis, Hebrides	Rev. Berners	Multi-humped
1897	Fai-tsi-long, Vietnam	Lieutenant Lagrésille and crew of the *Avalanche*	Multi-finned
1898 15 February	Fai-tsi-long, Vietnam	Lieutenant Lagrésille and crew of the *Avalanche*	Multi-finned
1898 24 February	Fai-tsi-long, Vietnam	Lieutenant Lagrésille and Commander Joannet, crews of the *Avalanche* and *Bayard*	Multi-finned
1898 11 July	Along Bay, Vietnam	Vice-Admiral de la Bonninière de Beaumont and Captain Boutet of the *Vaubin*	Multi-finned
1898	South Island, New Zealand	C. H. Tripp	Long-necked Seal
1900	Skye, Scotland	Sandy Campbell and others	Long-necked Seal
1900	Rhum, Scotland	Two men	Long-necked Seal
1901 May	Between New York and Belem	Captain Spedding and crew of the *Grangense*	Sea Saurian
1902 13 July	Ramhead, Victoria, Australia	Captain W. Firth and the crew of the *Chillagoe*	Multi-finned
1902 4 August	Oslofjord, Norway	Rev. Hans Davidsen and 10 others	Long-necked Seal
1903	Montrose, Scotland	Crew of the *Rosa*	Undefined Extension
1903 December	Tourane, Vietnam	Crew of the *Charles Hardouin*	Multi-finned
1903 December	Along Bay, Vietnam	Crew of the *Gueydon*	Multi-finned
1903	Hermanus, Cape Province, South Africa	Fishermen	Waterhorse

Year	Date	Location	Observer	Type
1904	12 February	Along Bay, Vietnam	Lieutenant Péron and crew of *Chateau-Renault*	Multi-finned
1904	14 February	Along Bay, Vietnam	Lieutenant L'Eost and crew of the *Décidée*	Multi-finned
1904	March	Along Bay, Vietnam	Crew of the *Gueydon*	Multi-finned
1904	July	Katwijk, Netherlands	P. W. Deems	Long-necked Seal
1904	22 October	Bab-el-Mandeb	Captain G. A. Zeilanga and crew of the *Ambon*	Sea Saurian
1905	13 April	Cape Horne	Captain P. Guillon of the *Rhône*	Long-necked Seal
1905	5 August	Wood Island, Maine, USA	General H. C. Merriam	Undefined Extension
1905	7 December	Paraiba, Brazil	Several people on *Valhalla*	Giant Eel
1906	?	Zandvoort, Netherlands	C. J. de B.	Long-necked Seal
1906	7 June	Zandvoort, Netherlands	Some workmen	Undefined Extension
1906	July	Katwijk, Netherlands	F. J. Knoops	Long-necked Seal
1906		Land's End, Cornwall	Officers of the *St Andrew*	Undefined Extension
1906	15 October	Gulf of Oman	Crew of the *Java*	Sea Saurian
1906	December	Saltsjobaden, Sweden	Victor Ankarcrona	Long-necked Seal
1907	26 April	Cork, Ireland	Sir Arthur Rostron and crew of the *Campania*	Long-necked Seal
1907	April	Bristol Channel, England	Mr M'Naughten	Long-necked Seal
1907	7 August	Padstow, Cornwall	Mrs J. C. Adkins and others	Long-necked Seal
1907		Katwijk, Netherlands	P. W. Deems	Long-necked Seal
1907	8 September	Surabaya, Java	Some Englishmen	Undefined Extension
1907		Gulf of Oman	Captain C. S. Visser and officers of the *Vondel*	Undefined Extension
1907	October	Porto, Corsica	Fishermen	Giant Eel
1908		Sognefjord, Norway	Dutch tourist	Undefined Extension
1908	June	Along Bay, Vietnam	Captain P. Merlees of the *Hanoi*	Multi-finned

123

Chronological Table of Sightings

Date	Location	Witnesses	Probable type
1909	China Sea ?	Captain Harbord and crew of the *Sultan*	Undefined Extension
1909	?	Vice-Admiral Robert H. Anstruther and crew of HMS *Caesar*	Long-necked Seal
1910	Connemara, Ireland	Howard St George and others	Long-necked Seal
1910	Meil Bay, Orkneys	W. J. Hutchinson and others	Long-necked Seal
1910 December	North Atlantic	Third officer of the *Potsdam*	Long-necked Seal
1910	Ingoy, Finmark, Norway	R. Eliassen	Scandinavian Giant Otter
1911	Côtes-du-Nord, France	F. Gélard and others	Long-necked Seal
1911	North Atlantic	Crew of the *Amsfeldijk*	Long-necked Seal
1911	Devon, England	William T. Cook and others	Giant Eel
1912 19 August	St Margaret's Bay, Kent, England	Mr Stone and others	Long-necked Seal
1912	Cape Matapan, Greece	Crew of the *Queen Eleanor*	Giant Eel
1912 July	Lowestoft, England	Rider Haggard's daughters	Long-necked Seal
1912 5 July	Devon, England	Captain Ruser of the *Kaiserin Augusta Viktoria*	Giant Eel
1912 August	Vancouver Island	Mrs H. Forbes	Waterhorse
1912 17 October	Gulf of Guinea	Mr John Fleming on the *Dover Castle*	Undefined Extension
1912	Portland, Maine, USA	Mrs F. W. Saunderson	Long-necked Seal
1913 20 April	Macquarie, Tasmania	Oscar Davies and W. Harris	Long-necked Seal
1913 30 August	Grand Bank, Newfoundland, Canada	Quartermaster and second officer of the *Corinthian*	Waterhorse
1913	Arabian Sea	John Scott Hughes	Long-necked Seal

1914		Oslofjord, Norway	W. E. Parkin and several others	Scandinavian Giant Otter
1915	30 July	French Atlantic coast	Commander G. G. F. von Forstner and crew of *U.28*	Sea Saurian
1916		Thasos, Greece	E. Plessis	Long-necked Seal
1919	?	San Clemente, California	Ralph Bandini and others	Waterhorse
1917	22 May	South of Iceland	Captain Dean and crew of HMS *Hilary*	Multi-humped
1917		Skye, Scotland	Mr Macdonald	Long-necked Seal
1918	28 July	North Sea	Commander Werner Lowisch and crew of *U.108*	Sea Saurian
1919	August	Hoy, Orkneys	J. Mackintosh Bell and several fishermen	Long-necked Seal
1920s		Natal, South Africa	Hugh Balance and others	Unclassifiable
1920	20 April	St Paul's Rocks, Atlantic	Thomas Muir, third officer of the *Tyne*	Long-necked Seal
1920	September	Fort Lauderdale, Florida	Crew of the *Craigsmere*	Multi-finned
1920		San Clemente, California	Ralph Bandini and Smith Warren	Waterhorse
1922	31 October	Ceylon	Officers of the *Bali*	Undefined Extension
1923	11 February	Somalia	Two officers of the *Mapia*	Multi-finned
1923	19 June	Loyalty Islands	Crew of the *Pacifique*	Waterhorse
1923	August	Channel Islands	Mrs Bromley and others	Waterhorse
1923		Black Deep, Thames, England	Captain Haselfoot and Commander Southern	Long-necked Seal
1923	22 September	Noumea, New Caledonia	Two native women	Waterhorse
1923	30 September	Noumea, New Caledonia	Mr Bailly	Waterhorse
1923	30 October	Costa Rica	Captain F. Van de Biesen and crew of the *India*	Undefined Extension

Date	Location	Witnesses	Probable type
1924 ?	Tuamotus	Ernest Davies and some other passengers of the *Noidoire*	Waterhorse
1924 6 May	Ajaccio, Corsica	G. Juranville	Undefined Extension
1925 2 February	Port Stephens, New South Wales	Captain R. Jaillard and crew of *Saint Francois Xavier*	Long-necked Seal
1925 23 July	Brisbane, Queensland, Australia	Captain P. De Haan and crew of the *Bawean*	Giant Eel
1925 ?	South China Sea	A. G. L. Jourdan	Giant Tadpole
1925	Menzies Bay, British Columbia	Jack Nord and others	Waterhorse
1925	North Sea, Lincolnshire	G.F.B.	Long-necked Seal
1926 21 January	Tulear, Madagascar	Dr Georges Petit	Multi-finned
1928 23 April	Cape Guardafui, Somalia	Some passengers on the *Oronsay*	Long-necked Seal
1928 15 August	Sumatra	Captain J. R. A. Swaan and crew of the *Bengkalis*	Long-necked Seal
1928	Vancouver Island, British Columbia	James Murray	Waterhorse
1928	Antikythera, Greece	Sir Arthur Conan Doyle and his wife	Long-necked Seal
1928	Isle of Man	Major W. P. Groves and others	Waterhorse
1928 September	New Caledonia	R. Reynell Bellamy	Long-necked Seal
1930s ?	Api, New Hebrides	A planter	Waterhorse
1930s ?	Noumea. New Caledonia	Captain of the *Euphrosyne*	Waterhorse
1930 June	Norfolk, England	L. M. Wilkes	Long-necked Seal
1930	Scarborough, New South Wales	?	Undefined Extension
1930 November	Cape Town, South Africa	Tromp van Diggelan on the *Dunbar Castle*	Long-necked Seal

Year	Date	Location	Observer	Classification
1930	?	Port Angeles, British Columbia	Rusty Beetle	Waterhorse
1931	June	Thorpeness, Suffolk	Mrs Sybil Armstrong	Long-necked Seal
1932		Between Sydney and Durban	Crew of the *Ceramic*	Giant Turtle
1932	10 August	Chatham Island, British Columbia	F. W. J. Kemp	Waterhorse
1933	?	British Columbia	Captain Walter Prengle of the *Santa Lucia*	Waterhorse
1933	?	British Columbia	Captain Arthur Slater of the *Princess Joan*	Waterhorse
1933	?	British Columbia	Captain W. H. Davies	Waterhorse
1933	?	British Columbia	Percy Barnes	Waterhorse
1933	7 July	Natal, South Africa	G. P. Court and others	Giant Eel
1933	1 October	Chatham Island, British Columbia	Major W. H. Langley	Waterhorse
1933	4 October	Chatham Island, British Columbia	R. C. Ross	Waterhorse
1933	April	Indian Ocean	Mrs Lillian Rawlings on the *Chitral*	Long-necked Seal
1934	January	Querqueville, France	Skipper of *Tug 117*	Long-necked Seal
1934	30 January	St Eustatius, Lesser Antilles	Crew and passengers on the *Mauritania*	Long-necked Seal
1934	28 February	Filey Brig, England	Wilkinson Herbert	Long-necked Seal
1934	March	Nassau, Bahamas	Crew and passengers on the *Mauritania*	Multi-finned
1934	July	Azores	Captain Maguerez of the *Cuba*	Long-necked Seal
1934	August	Townsville, Queensland, Australia	Robert E. Steele	Giant Eel
1934	18 August	Townsville, Queensland, Australia	Oscar Swanson and others	Unclassifiable

Chronological Table of Sightings

Date		Location	Witnesses	Probable type
1934	25 August	Bowen, Queensland, Australia	Mr Hurst and others	Multi-finned
1934		Townsville, Queensland, Australia	3 fishing parties	Multi-finned
1934		Great Barrier Reef	Crew of the *Rehata*	Unclassifiable
1934		Vineyard Sound, Mass., USA	Thomas Ratcliffe	Giant Eel
1934		Pender Island, British Columbia	Cyril Andrews	Waterhorse
1935		Norfolk, Virginia, USA	Lieutenant Hogan of the *Elektra*	Multi-finned
1936	August	Norfolk, England	Mr Enkel and others	Long-necked Seal
1936	5 August	Norfolk, England	H. T. Witard and others	Long-necked Seal
1937		Pentland Skerries, Scotland	J. R. Brown	Long-necked Seal
1937	26 October	St Thomas, Virgin Islands	G. Cooper on the *Amerika*	Long-necked Seal
1937		Sunset Beach, British Columbia	F. B. Lawrence and others	Waterhorse
1937	?	Trusthorpe, Lincolnshire	R. W. Midgely	Multi-humped
1938		Easington, Yorkshire	Mrs Joan Borgeest	Waterhorse
1938	21 October	Southwold, Suffolk	Ernest Watson and others	Long-necked Seal
1939		Côtes-du-Nord, France	A. F. Waymark and others	Long-necked Seal
1939	July	Firth of Forth, Scotland	Fishermen	Waterhorse
1939		Astoria, Oregon, USA	Fishing Crews	Waterhorse
1939	?	Nova Scotia, Canada	Charles Ballard	Giant Eel
1942		Vancouver Island, British Columbia	?	Waterhorse

128

1943	March	St Andrews Bay, Florida	Thomas Helm and wife	Waterhorse
1943		Vancouver Island, British Columbia	Ernest Lee	Waterhorse
1944		Gulf of Guinea	Second Officer J. Drummond of the *Buster*	Giant Eel
1945	August	Hilston, Yorkshire	B. M. Bayliss	Multi-humped
1945		Canala, New Caledonia	A. Fere and others	Long-necked Seal
1946	7 November	California, USA	Many witnesses	Unclassifiable
1946		Queen Charlotte Islands, British Columbia	Captain House	Long-necked Seal
1946	?	Gower Peninsula, Wales	A. G. Thompson	Waterhorse
1947		Vancouver Island, British Columbia	Peter Pantages and a taxi driver	Waterhorse
1947		Security Bay, Alaska	Mr and Mrs Lou Baggon on the *Suntrana*	Waterhorse
1947	8 May	Pennock Island, Alaska	Lauri Carlson and L. Panama	Waterhorse
1947	August	Durban, Natal, South Africa	Crew of tug *Harry Cheadle*	Waterhorse
1947	September	Isipingo, South Africa	J. Kennedy	Multi-humped
1947	4 September	Boston, Mass., USA	John Ruhl	Multi-humped
1947	November	Vancouver Island, British Columbia	G. W. Saggers	Waterhorse
1947	30 December	North Carolina, USA	Crew of *Santa Clara*	Giant Eel
1950	5 February	Vancouver Island, British Columbia	Judge J. T. Brown	Waterhorse
1950		Cliftonville, Kent, England	John Handley	Long-necked Seal
1950	December	Summerland, California	Opal Lambert	Waterhorse
1953	13 February	Qualicum, British Columbia	Frank Waterfall	Long-necked Seal
1953	8 June	San Clemente, California	Sam Randazzo and his crew	Waterhorse

Date		Location	Witnesses	Probable type
1953	August	Firth of Clyde, Scotland	Fishermen	Long-necked Seal
1954	24 February	Vancouver Island, British Columbia	Several people	Waterhorse
1954	25 February	Vancouver Island, British Columbia	W. Baldwin and others	Waterhorse
1954	21 July	Argyllshire, Scotland	Eric Robinson	Long-necked Seal
1954		La Jolla, California	Phil Parker and others	Unclassifiable
1955	6 June	Nova Scotia, Canada	Crew of the *Rhapsody*	Giant Turtle
1957		Mass., USA	Crew of the *Noreen*	Multi-humped
1958	February	Rio de Janeiro	Ferreira de Rocha and others	Long-necked Seal
1958	29 April	Puget Sound, Washington	Rev. J. Oosterhuff	Waterhorse
1958	August	Calabria, Italy	Several tourists	Giant Eel
1958	August	East London, South Africa	Crew of the *Golden Flame*	Waterhorse
1959	13 September	Soay, Hebrides	Tex Geddes and others	Giant Turtle
1960	1 January	Brisbane, Australia	Ron Spencer and others	Waterhorse
1960	January	Brisbane, Australia	Nigel Tutt and others	Waterhorse
1960	26 December	Sydney, British Columbia	A couple	Waterhorse
1961	?	South of the Philippines	O. D. Rasmussen and his family on the *Taiyuen*	Long-necked Seal
1961	?	Finmark, Norway	Captain Sune and Finn Devold of the *Johan Jhort*	Undefined Extension
1962		Helensborough, Scotland	Jack Hay	Long-necked Seal
1962	13 February	Vancouver Island, British Columbia	Alan Maclean and others	Waterhorse
1962	September	Queensland, Australia	R. Duncan	Long-necked Seal
1962	9 October	Queensland, Australia	R. Duncan	Long-necked Seal

			R. Guy and others	Waterhorse
1962	28 December	Vancouver Island, British Columbia		Multi-humped
1963	13 February	Vopnafjorther, Iceland	A. and S. Jonsson	Multi-humped
1963	July	Off New York	Dr. L. A. Walford and crew of the *Challenger*	Unclassifiable
1963	August	Cardigan Bay, Wales	P. Sharman	Long-necked Seal
1964	12 May	Nantucket, Mass., USA	Crew of the *Blue Sea*	Multi-humped
1964	May	Nantucket, Mass., USA	Crew of the *Friendship*	Multi-humped
1964		Grand Rhône, France	J. Borelli and his son	Undefined Extension
1964	June	Jura, Hebrides	Neil and Lily Macinnes	Waterhorse
1965	21 June	Ardnamurchan, Scotland	Mrs Lilian Lowe and others	Long-necked Seal
1966	25 July	Mid-North Atlantic	Captain John Ridgway and Sergeant Chay Blyth in *English Rose III*	Undefined Extension
1966	October	Skegness, Lincolnshire	George and May Ashton	Multi-humped
1975	September	Pendennis Point, Cornwall	Mrs Scott and Mr Riley	Long-necked Seal
1976	January	Rosemullion Head, Cornwall	Duncan Viner	Long-necked Seal
1976	January	Rosemullion Head, Cornwall	Amelia Johnson	Long-necked Seal
1976	January	Mouth of the Helford River, Cornwall	Gerald Bennet	Long-necked Seal
1976	March	Trefusis Point, Cornwall	Mary F	Long-necked Seal
1976	May	Mouth of the Helford River, Cornwall	Tony Rogers and John Chambers	Long-necked Seal
1976	August	Falmouth Bay, Cornwall	George Vinnicombe	Long-necked Seal
1976	17 November	Mouth of the Helford River, Cornwall	David Clarke and Tony 'Doc' Shiels	Long-necked Seal

131

Bibliography

Details of sightings included in the chronological list but not described in this book may be found in those publications marked with an asterisk.

Cousteau, J., and Diole, P., *Octopus and Squid — The Soft Intelligence,* Cassell, London, 1973.

Dinsdale, T., *The Leviathans,* Futura, London, 1976.*

Gould, R. T., *The Case for the Sea Serpent,* Phillip Allen, London, 1930.*

Heuvelmans, B., *In the Wake of the Sea Serpents,* Hart-Davis, London, 1968.*

Keel, J. A., *Strange Creatures from Time and Space,* Neville Spearman, London, 1975.*

Mackal, R. P., *The Monsters of Loch Ness,* Futura, London, 1976.

Norman, J. R., *Great Fishes, Whales and Dolphins,* Norton, New York, 1938.

Oudemans, A. C., *The Great Sea Serpent,* Luzac, London, 1892.*

Romer, A. S., *Man and the Vertebrates,* Penguin Books, Harmondsworth, 1970.

Romer, A. S., *Vertebrate Palaeontology,* University of Chicago Press, 1945.

Smith, J. L. B., *Old Fourlegs — The Story of the Coelacanth,* Longmans, Green, London 1956.

Swinton, W. E., *Giants Past and Present,* Robert Hale, London, 1966.

Young, J. Z., *The Life of Vertebrates,* Oxford University Press, 1962.

For Product Safety Concerns and Information please contact our EU
representative GPSR@taylorandfrancis.com
Taylor & Francis Verlag GmbH, Kaufingerstraße 24, 80331 München, Germany

www.ingramcontent.com/pod-product-compliance
Lightning Source LLC
Chambersburg PA
CBHW050529270326
41926CB00015B/3134

9 780367 077358